# RATIONAL FAITH

# RATIONAL
## *faith*

*A Philosopher's Defence of Christianity*

STEPHEN T. DAVIS

LION

Published by Lion Books
an imprint of
**Lion Hudson plc**
Wilkinson House, Jordan Hill Road,
Oxford OX2 8DR, England
www.lionhudson.com/lion

ISBN 978 0 7459 8006 5
e-ISBN 978 0 7459 8007 2

First published by InterVarsity Press, P.O. Box 1400, Downers Grove, IL 60515-1426,
ivpress.com, email@ivpress.com

**Acknowledgments**
Scripture quotations, unless otherwise noted, are from the New Revised Standard
Version of the Bible, copyright 1989 by the Division of Christian Education of the
National Council of the Churches of Christ in the USA. Used by permission. All rights
reserved.

Chapter Three based on "The Gospels are Reliable as Historically Factual Accounts" by
Stephen T. Davis from *Debating Christian Theism*, edited by Moreland, J.P., Sweis, K.A. &
Meister, C.V. (2013). Used by permission of Oxford University Press.

While many stories in this book are true, some names and identifying information may
have been changed to protect the privacy of individuals.

A catalogue record for this book is available from the British Library

Printed and bound in the UK, January 2017, LH26

To the memory of my beloved wife, Charis

(February 1941–March 2000)

# CONTENTS

# INTRODUCTION

Years ago, as a soon-to-be high school graduate, I had an interesting conversation with a lay leader in the congregation I attended. He knew I was a fairly recent convert to Christianity. He had a word of advice for me: "Whatever you do," he said, "in college do not major in philosophy. Lots of Christian students take a class in philosophy and then lose their faith."

Despite my respect for the man, his advice struck me as odd. I had no clear idea at that point what philosophy was, although I knew it had something to do with thinking hard. But I remember saying to myself that if Christianity is true—as I believed it was—Christians ought to be able to answer any questions and stand up to any objections that critics from philosophy (or anywhere else) might raise. So I tucked the man's suggestion into some remote corner of my mind and went ahead with my plans for college. Little did I then know that I would later minor in philosophy (I discovered philosophy too late in my academic career to major in it), earn a PhD in philosophy and spend my career as a professor of philosophy.

I have spent virtually my entire adult life teaching at secular institutions of higher learning. Accordingly, I am quite familiar with the kinds of intellectual and academic challenges that Christian college students face at such institutions. Over the years I have had many conversations with Christian students who are struggling with something they were taught in not just philosophy classes but classes in psychology, biology, sociology, religious studies, physics and many other disciplines.

This book is about those difficulties. I want to say some things about what I take to be several of the major intellectual challenges that Christian students face in contemporary academia. They revolve around questions such as these: Is there any such thing as objective truth? Why believe in God? Is the Bible's picture of Jesus reliable? Was Jesus really raised from the dead? Does evolution disprove Christianity? Can't purported religious experiences be explained by neuroscience? Aren't other religions equally valid as Christianity? Don't evil and suffering show that God does not exist? Can we be perfectly happy apart from God?

Of course Christian students face other sorts of issues in today's university culture. Many of them are more behavioral than intellectual challenges. I am thinking of the temptations of the easy availability, and even social pressure to succumb to, binge drinking, drug use and casual sex. But in this book I am not going to address those sorts of concerns. This book is about academic challenges to Christian faith.

The bottom line is that today in American secular colleges and universities Christian students (as well as Christian professors) often have a difficult time. In many ways the university gives them the impression that their religious beliefs are outmoded, superstitious and naive, and that their ethical views are old fashioned, oppressive and enslaving. The secular world thinks that Christians are inflexibly dogmatic about their beliefs and major in condemning other people.

This book is mainly aimed at two sorts of persons: (1) Christian academics, especially those who are located at secular universities and colleges, who are troubled by the kinds of issues discussed here. This includes philosophers, people in religious studies and those who are located in other disciplines. (2) But it is primarily aimed at students, both undergraduate and graduate students, who are Christians or are considering Christianity, and who also wonder about the issues discussed here. My hope is that this book can be of help to people in both groups.

A few of the chapters of this book, or earlier versions of them, have appeared elsewhere. But most of them have not appeared in print before. I wish to thank those friends who are mentioned in the concluding notes of chapters three, five and six. Most of all, I want to thank my Claremont McKenna College colleague and friend Eric Yang, who read and helpfully commented on the entire manuscript.

# IS THERE ANY SUCH THING
# AS OBJECTIVE TRUTH?

Right at the outset of this book, we need to consider the concept of truth.[1] This is because there are many in academia today who reject, in one way of another, the notion of objective truth. I actually believe that the validity of everything anyone does, in academic studies or in ordinary life, depends on objective truth. This of course includes Christian faith. I will explain why.

## Why This Topic Is Important

One reason why I want to begin with this issue is this: over the years I have spoken at many Christian colleges and universities. And I have noticed, especially among some of the younger professors, some confusion on issues of truth. These scholars were Christians, of course, but they did not know how or whether you could reconcile Christian commitment with the epistemological and moral relativism espoused by many of their secular professors in graduate school. In some degree or other, I suspect, all Christian academics these days struggle with this issue. And so do many Christian undergraduates.

Here is a brief road map of where I will go in this chapter. First I want to define two theories of truth, objective truth and relative truth. I will speak about both epistemological and moral relativism. Then I will try to defend a realist or objective notion of truth against two criticisms frequently raised against it. Next, I will raise several criticisms of relativism. I think the theory can be refuted on purely philosophical grounds (i.e., without bringing in theological considerations). But then I will turn explicitly to Christian concerns about truth and especially to Jesus' claim to be "the truth." My final substantive point will be that morality requires God. I will even offer an argument for the existence of God based on morality. In conclusion, I will briefly exegete two texts from Proverbs that I think are relevant to the struggles of Christians in academia.

## Realist Theories of Truth

What then does it mean to call a statement true? Or, as Pilate cynically asked Jesus, "What is truth?" (John 18:38).

There are of course different senses of the word *true*. We use expressions like "true blue," "true north" and being "true to yourself." But I am asking about the epistemological or cognitive sense of the word, the sense that concerns the truth or falsity of statements or claims. And there exists a classic answer to Pilate's question, which is found in both Plato and Aristotle. We can call this answer the *realist* notion of truth. Its central idea is that a statement is true if and only if what the statement says to be the case is the case. So truth has to do with the relationship between the statements that we make and the reality that exists external to them. Or, as Thomas Aquinas famously put it, "truth is the agreement between the idea and the thing."[2] And if a given statement does agree with reality in this way, then on the realist notion of truth the statement is objectively true.

One way of trying to spell out that relationship is the so-called *correspondence* theory of truth. It says that a statement is true if it corresponds to the facts. If I say to you on a Tuesday that "today is Sunday" or (on any day) that "San Francisco is south of Los Angeles," those statements are false because what they say does not correspond to the way things are.

The correspondence theory has come in for criticism over the centuries. I will mention two objections. The first—which I am only going to state but not discuss—is that nobody has ever spelled out exactly what *correspondence* is, what exactly it is for a statement to correspond to or with a fact. I think this criticism is largely well-taken. This is work that remains for correspondence theorists to do.

But the second criticism—which is much in the spirit of our age, as you will see—is one I want to respond to. The objection says that we do not have unmediated access to "the facts." That is, on the correspondence theory we could only test a truth claim if we could be directly confronted with bare facts (i.e., confronted apart from our language and conceptual schemes). Take the statement "There is a lamp on the table." To see whether there is correspondence here—so the critics say—we would have to know the facts, quite independently of our language. That is, we would have to be able to know whether there is a lamp on the table quite apart from our ideas and words. And that is something—so this criticism runs—we cannot do.

But I do not think this criticism holds. We might not have any *unmediated access to facts* (i.e., access unaffected by our ideas, conceptual schemes and words). But we do have *access to facts*, and that is the crucial point. By various means we can check on whether there is a lamp on the table. We can look and see; we can ask somebody who is in a position to know; we can read a description of the furniture of the room written by somebody we trust. If we could not recognize facts about the world that exists "out there" (i.e., external to our minds)—for example, that a train is coming toward us or that a steep cliff is one step away—we would not survive. We might as well lie down and die.

But even if this criticism of the correspondence theory is telling, it will not matter for our purposes in the present chapter. The criticism has no force against the objective notion of truth: that theory only aims to say what truth is, not to provide ways of determining what is true and what is false. Again, it simply says that a statement is true if what it claims to be the case is in fact the case. That is the notion that I want to argue for.

### Relativism on Truth

But unfortunately there is a much more serious threat on the horizon, one that endangers both the correspondence theory and all realist or objective notions of truth. This is a theory known as relativism. I will get to relativism by first talking about one way of arriving there—namely, via postmodernism.

Postmodernism as an academic theory has pretty much shot its wad by now, but aspects of it remain influential. As I understand them, postmodernists make four crucial points. First, they reject the Enlightenment model of reason, science and the scientific method as the ideal vehicles for gaining knowledge. Second, they emphasize the point that all persons have social locations, so all claims are located by nation, gender, race and class. In short, there is no "view from nowhere." Everybody has a location that influences and biases what he or she believes; there is no complete objectivity to view reality from. Third, postmodernists emphasize issues of power; all knowledge claims are political. To claim to know something is to attempt to exercise influence and power over others. Fourth, postmodernists are known for the slogan "Everything is a text." Every use of language, and indeed every physical object, is subject to various interpretations; there is no one intrinsic or objective meaning to any text or thing. No one metanarrative (i.e., no one overarching scheme of meaning) can have total dominance.

What does this have to do with objective theories of truth? Well, the logic of postmodernism leads directly to what its defenders call contextualization. Truth is internal to contexts; beliefs are true and false in relation to various social locations; beliefs are justified socially. This then is a version of relativism.

Let's define *relativism* as the view that the truth or falsity of claims depends on who is making or evaluating them. A proposition like "Murder is morally wrong" can be true for one person and false for another. There is no such thing as transpersonal, transcontextual truths. There is no "God's eye view" of things. And all truth claims are true for the people who are sincerely making them. If I think that murder is morally wrong, I am correct. And if you think murder is morally right, you are correct. What is true is always "true for you," but not necessarily for anybody else.

This theory is in direct contrast to the realist or objective notion of truth. On that venerable theory, if something is true, it is true no matter what anybody may think. If it is true that "San Francisco is north of Los Angeles," then that statement is true even if there are people who do not understand the statement or even if there are people who think it false.

But three caveats are in order in order to avoid misunderstanding. First, no defender of objective theories of truth will deny the obvious fact that there are many statements whose truth value— that is, whether they are true or false—we do not or even cannot know. This fact alone ought to lead to a kind of epistemological humility. There are lots of things that we do not know, and we may be mistaken even on many of the points where we have firm opinions. Second, the truth values of some statements change over time. If I say, "I am standing," I can change the truth value of that statement from true to false by simply sitting down. And third, there are some areas in life where relativism appears to be true. Which tastes better, steak or pizza? Who is the better composer, J. S. Bach or Paul McCartney? On such issues (i.e., on matters of taste) you and I can disagree and we can both be correct, since we are simply reporting our own preferences. But on most matters (e.g., on whether San Francisco is north of Los Angeles) I claim that relativism is simply false. Let me explain why.

Notice that relativism in truth leads immediately to relativism in ethics. If all truth is socially located and varies from person to person, then, obviously, statements like "Murder is morally wrong" are only relatively true. Nothing is morally right or wrong per se; some things are (as relativists say) right or wrong "for you."

I confess that I have never clearly understood what the expression "true for you" is supposed to mean. If somebody says (as a student of mine once said to me), "Christianity is true for you but not for me," I think that just means "You are a Christian and I am not." That is, we disagree. And I submit that what we disagree about is this: Is Christianity *true* (i.e., objectively true)?

Indeed, there is a deep incoherence in most versions of relativism. We see it most clearly in the attempt to argue that nothing is objectively true. The very claim "Nothing is objectively true" is certainly pushed by most relativists as if *it* were objectively true. Thus their theory is self-refuting, like the position of the person who says, "I am unable to speak a single word of English." And if relativists deny that the statement "Nothing is objectively true" is meant by them to be objectively true (i.e., if they insist that it is merely their own perspective on things), that raises the question why those of us who think that there *are* statements that are objectively true should agree with them or even take their theory seriously.

Moreover, there is this question: How can we be sure that we have not been biased by our social location in making the very claim that our social location always distorts our ability to access reality? I have never heard a relativist satisfactorily answer that question. It is quite true, of course, that we all have locations, and it is true that our locations influence what we believe. In today's academic world, we have to take those points seriously. But neither point rules out the possibility that we can have objectively true beliefs.

Here is a personal impression from years of teaching American college students. We professors used to see loads of students arriving at college who seemed committed to a kind of poorly thought-through ethical relativism. But then, slowly but noticeably, that seemed to stop, almost as if somebody had turned off a spigot. I think a certain historical event was partially responsible—namely, the 9/11 attacks. After that event I think many young people at least implicitly decided that although Mohamed Atta and his cohorts may have sincerely believed that what they were doing was morally right, their acts were morally wrong. And the minute you embrace that thought, you are no relativist.

But despite the arguments I've been giving, some people might feel that there is still something wrong with objectivism—namely, that it leads to intolerance. Indeed, I think what motivates most relativists is the desire to be tolerant. The idea, I guess, is this: given that people strongly disagree about important things and are sometimes even willing to resort to violence over them, the best way to promote the moral value that we call tolerance is to insist that there is no such thing as objective truth. That way there are no absolute truths for people to get dogmatic about.

But that idea is badly misguided. There is no necessary connection between being an objectivist on truth and being intolerant. Of course, there is a *historical* tendency that can be disturbing—a sense of absolute certainty does lead some people to intolerance and imperialism. Still, relativists who try to make this point don't seem to realize that there can be moral systems that are taken to be objectively true and that teach or even require tolerance.

I too strongly believe in tolerance. No sensible person can read the newspaper or the Internet or watch the news on television without realizing the need for people of divergent views to get along. The Christian motivation for tolerance is not that nobody has the objective truth but that Jesus told us to love all people and especially our enemies. And we Christians try to practice tolerance and respect for people precisely because we believe that Jesus' teaching is true (i.e., objectively true).

You can see, then, that contrary to what relativists sometimes say in their quest for tolerance, there is no necessary connection whatsoever between believing in objective truth and being fanatical, dogmatic, inflexible, narrow-minded or unwilling to debate. Here, I think, we are at the heart of secular academia's suspicion of objective truth. But tolerance is not holding that all viewpoints are equally valid; I am pointing out that you can be an objectivist on truth and still treat other people with respect even if you think their views are objectively false.

Truth is characterized by four things. First, truth is objective. The truth of the true statements we make is not internal to us; it lies in the world. What makes a statement true is not our subjective feelings about it but the way the world is. Second, truth is universal. The true statements that we make are true not just "for us" but for all people. Third, truth is lasting. As we have seen, some statements can change in truth value because the world changes, but the truth of a true statement is eternally the same unless the world does change. Truth is enduring, not ephemeral. Fourth, truth makes it possible for us to communicate, survive and thrive. It is true that it is good to step out of the way of oncoming traffic and to eat a balanced diet. We could not survive apart from those sorts of truths.

I would sum up all four points by saying that truth is *trustworthy*. As opposed to feelings, tastes and beliefs that are "true for you," truth can be relied on.

## Jesus as the Truth

I now turn to the relationship between truth and Christianity. In the Gospel of John, Jesus says, "I am the way, the truth, and the life. No one comes to the Father except through me" (John 14:6). What did Jesus mean when he said that he was "the truth"? What do we Christians mean when we make the same affirmation about him?

I submit that we mean three things. The meaning here is clearly different from, although related to, the epistemological sense of truth we have been discussing thus far. First, Jesus is "the truth" in that what he says is objectively true. The teachings of Jesus as we find them in the Gospels are authoritative for us; our job is to submit to them, to take them as words from God. We do our best to follow them; we model our lives on them; we allow Jesus' teachings to shape and mold us. As Jesus himself said, "My words will not pass away" (Matthew 24:35).

Second, Jesus is "the truth" in that what he did on our behalf is the true route to redemption and wholeness in life. Jesus is not just a guru who issues profound and helpful teachings about life, like Socrates or Confucius. Jesus is the Savior, the one who by his life, death and resurrection made it possible for our sins to be forgiven and for us to know God.

Third, Jesus is "the truth" in that he truly was and is the Son of God (i.e., God incarnate). I think the resurrection of Jesus from the dead was a way for God to repeat in action what he had said in words at Jesus' baptism, "This is my Son, the Beloved, with whom I am well pleased" (Matthew 3:17). There are very many gurus and spiritual leaders in the world: Which of them should we trust? If Jesus is simply a guru, then no matter how helpful his teachings are, they can be rejected on grounds such as, "Well, I like my guru better than your guru." But if Jesus is the Son of God, then there is a non-gainsayable finality about what he said, what he did and who he was. He was indeed "the way" to God. As he said, "No one comes to the Father except through me."

Notice that all three of these points—that what Jesus said, did and claimed to be were true—require a robust notion of truth. Of course a relativist (a confused one, I submit) could be a Christian in the sense of passionately choosing to follow Jesus despite the belief that Christianity is only true "for him or her." And certainly Jesus may be attractive to some people and not to others. But what we Christians need to affirm of Jesus, as the villagers of Sychar said, is that "this is truly the Savior of the world" (John 4:42). So I contend that Christians need an objective notion of truth to undergird our deepest theological commitments.

## Why Morality Needs God

I want to make one more point about moral relativism. If there are no objective values but only good and bad "for you" and good and bad "for me," then there is no rational or trustworthy basis for defending the ideals and accomplishments of human civilization at its best. These would be achievements like the equality of all people before the law, government as based on the consent of the people, tolerance of and civility toward those who disagree with us, freedom of speech, and freedom of religion. If there are no objective values, then the only available goals are the targets of one's own desires, and the only available vehicles for convincing people are power and politics.

I once had a conversation in the faculty mail room with a colleague who was a strong feminist, a historian I liked and respected. She was president of one of the national organizations for academic women. She and I were discussing violence against women. I had always been genuinely puzzled why so many academic feminists—who I agreed with on many other points— buy into relativism and use it in their work, as indeed she did. I told her that in my opinion the strongest thing that a relativist can say against violence against women is, "Violence against women is morally wrong according to me and my group." But that of course allows the rapist to say, "Sorry, but my group does not accept that standard." So I asked my colleague, "Don't you want to say to the rapist: 'What you are doing is just plain morally wrong, no matter what you or anybody may think'?" And the odd thing was that she then looked at me for about thirty seconds without being able to think of what to say in reply. The fact is, she was torn. To her great credit, she wanted to agree with me that violence against women is just plain wrong, whatever rapists may think, but her methodological commitment to relativism made that impossible.

I tell this story not to try to show how clever I was or how dumb she was. My friend was not a philosopher, and quite understandably had probably never before thought about the issues in just this way. I tell it to illustrate the dilemma that academics today face. In many ways, her problem is our problem.

I want to argue that objective values—that is, truths in a realist sense in the area of morality—require God. But first I want to be clear on what I am not claiming. I am not denying that atheists or agnostics can be morally good people. I have many such colleagues in Claremont who are just that. I am not saying that atheists and agnostics cannot know what is right and what is wrong. Of course many of them do. I am not saying that atheists and agnostics cannot make moral decisions. Of course they can. I am not saying that atheists and agnostics cannot formulate a good ethical system. I think they can do that.

What I *am* saying is that only if God exists is there a secure rational basis for objective right and wrong, for moral accountability and for moral obligation. Now I must admit to you that I am very much swimming against the philosophical tide at this point: there have been many famous attempts to base morality on something other than God. Utilitarianism is one example; Kant's ethical system is another. And I don't want to argue against them on this occasion. But my belief is that God's holy and perfectly good nature constitutes the objective standard of right and wrong, and is the source of moral values. And God's commands to human beings constitute the source of moral obligation. In the Christian faith the essence of morality is the twofold commandment that we (1) love the Lord our God with all our heart and mind and strength, and (2) love our neighbor as ourselves.

But if there is no God, morality is merely a human invention or a byproduct of biological and cultural evolution, and is accordingly entirely subjective and relativistic. Morals are either expressions of personal taste or else devices to help us adapt and thrive as organisms. I can tell you that there are notable philosophers and thinkers, some of them atheists, who are prepared to concede the point that I am making.

For example, Max Horkheimer, a twentieth-century German philosopher of the Frankfurt School, writes, "Without God one will try in vain to preserve absolute meaning."[3] And Canadian philosopher Kai Nielsen writes,

> We have not been able to show that reason requires the
> moral point of view, or that all really rational persons should

not be individual egoists or classical amoralists. Reason doesn't decide here. The picture I have painted for you is not a pleasant one. Reflection on it depresses me.... Pure practical reason, even with a good knowledge of the facts, will not take you to morality.[4]

And Richard Taylor, a philosophical ethicist, writes, "Contemporary writers in ethics, who blithely discourse upon right and wrong and moral obligation without any reference to religion, are really just weaving intellectual webs from thin air; which amounts to saying that they discourse without meaning."[5] In other words, there is no rational basis for objective moral standards apart from God.[6]

A second point: without God there is no good reason for me to do the morally good thing when I can benefit from doing the wrong thing and can do it with impunity. If morality is simply a function of where the human race has evolved thus far, this, as I say, is a flimsy basis for the affirmation of values like the dignity and worth of all persons, the need to treat people as ends in themselves, and the duty to do the moral thing even in situations when you can get away with doing the immoral thing.

But can I give an argument for the existence of God based on morality? Yes, I can. I'll call it "the genocide argument for the existence of God." We can define *genocide* as the crime of intentionally destroying or trying to destroy an entire group of people, usually a racial, ethnic, national or religious group. My argument presupposes moral objectivism—that is, the theory that certain things are morally right (things like compassion, truth telling and promise keeping) and that certain other things (things like lying, cruelty and murder) are morally wrong. It also assumes that genocide is one of the things that is morally wrong.

Here is how the argument goes:

1. Genocide is a departure from the way that things ought to be.

2. If genocide is a departure from the way that things ought to be, then there is a way that things ought to be.

3. If there is a way that things ought to be, then there is a design plan for things.

4. If there is a design plan for things, then there is an author of the plan, a designer.

5. This designer we can call God.[7]

A full design plan would simply be a list of all those things that are morally right, that constitute the way that things ought to be, and a list of all the things that ought not to be.

Obviously, the genocide argument does not prove that God has all the properties that we Christians think God has. It does not prove that God is omniscient or omnipotent or a Trinity, for example. Still, there can be no such thing as an authorless design plan, a plan for how things ought to be that follows merely from how things are.

*Science* is our word for the discovery of how the world is. But nothing science can discover about how the world *is* tells us anything about how it *ought to be*. Accordingly, the designer must be a sentient being. That sentient being is obviously not anyone who is reading this chapter or indeed any human being, so it is surely God.

## Teaching Truth

It used to be said, in the pre-postmodernism days, that the purpose of university research is to discover new knowledge, and the purpose of university education is to teach what we know to students. From my younger days I can certainly remember talk like that in speeches by university administrators or in commencement addresses. Those sorts of ideas would sound, at best, quaint and even ill-informed in our day.

Still, the idea that we are to teach our students what is true has appeal to me. Proverbs 3:1-2 says, "My child, do not forget my teaching, / but let your heart keep my commandments." Clearly this advice is addressed to young people; it begins with "My child." By using the phrase, "my teachings," the writer of the proverb was undoubtedly urging obedience to God's teachings, not his own. Otherwise, the next line would make no sense: "for length of days and years of life / and abundant welfare they will give you." Only God can bestow gifts like that.

Please recall the point I made earlier: truth is objective, universal, lasting and helpful. Now note that in John 17, in Jesus' high-priestly prayer, Jesus says to the Father, "Your word is truth" (John 17:17). And if God's word is true, then the truth of God from the Scriptures has the same four characteristics. First, it is objective. As God says through Isaiah: "I the LORD speak the truth" (Isaiah 45:19). If truth is what is spoken by God, and if God is omniscient, then the truth that God speaks is not just what God believes but what is objectively true. Second, it is universal. In Acts 17 Luke compliments the Jews of Beroea because when Paul preached to them, they diligently searched the Scriptures "to see whether these things were so" (Acts 17:11). They wanted to know whether Paul's teachings were universally true, not just attractive to them. Third, it is eternal. As the psalmist said to God, "The sum of your word is truth; / and every one of your righteous ordinances endures forever" (Psalm 119:160; cf. Psalm 40:7-8). Fourth, it is redemptive. As Jesus said, "You will know the truth, and the truth will make you free" (John 8:32).

Earlier, I summed up these points by saying that truth is trustworthy. And the same thing is true here: Jesus is trustworthy. He can be relied on. He is the Savior.

I think there is no higher calling in life than to teach people the truth of God's teachings. Truth is the heart of what Christian academics do. One of these divine teachings is found in the sublime words of Proverbs 3:5-6:

> Trust in the LORD with all your heart,
>     and do not rely on your own insight.
> In all your ways acknowledge him,
>     and he will make straight your paths.

Whether they are adults or college students, those who acknowledge God in all their ways are not only believing but are doing the truth.

# WHY BELIEVE IN GOD?

Let us stipulate that the word *God* means a unique, all-powerful, all-knowing and loving Creator of the heavens and the earth. So *theists* are people who believe that God exists; *atheists* are people who believe that God does not exist; and *agnostics* are people who have neither belief.

There is no doubt that one of the primary intellectual challenges theists face—maybe the biggest challenge—is the question why any sensible person would believe in God. Why should anybody believe in something that cannot be seen or measured or touched or proved?

I will begin with some thoughts about why I personally believe in God. The primary historical reason is doubtless the fact that my parents believed in God and taught me to do the same. Although my family was not particularly religious, my mom and dad did believe in God and occasionally took us to church, and as a child I naturally accepted the idea that God exists.

But since many people grow up to reject opinions held by their parents, I should add this important phrase: and I have never encountered any convincing reason to reject belief in God. Like everybody else, I have listened over the years to very many reasons that atheists give against God, but I have never found any of them to be convincing. There are of course serious antitheistic arguments that theists must think about and treat carefully, but I think many of them amount to sheer ranting or even hand waving. They are often of the form "After all, everybody knows that _____" or "Of course every intelligent person today realizes that _____." Richard Dawkins's book *The God Delusion*, for example, is full of more bluster than argumentation, and when he gets to producing arguments, they are often painfully weak.[1]

## Subjective Reasons for Belief in God

But by far the most important reason why I believe in God is this: I have had experiences in my life that I naturally find myself interpreting in terms of the presence of God. I have experienced what I take to be God's protection, God's guidance, God's challenges and God's mercy. These experiences are important aspects of my life.

But both of the reasons I have just given are, as we might say, subjective. Nobody else feels any need to accept what my parents taught me, and nobody else has experienced my encounters with God. Accordingly, you might wonder whether I am able to give any objective evidence for God—an argument, perhaps. Accordingly, in addition to the argument about God and morality that I made in chapter one, I will suggest two of them here.

## The Sort of World We Live In

My first argument has to do with the kind of world we live in. There are two possible explanations of the existence of our world. One possibility is that the world is entirely accidental or just has no explanation; the world has always been here and so was not created. The second possibility is that the world was brought into existence by some sort of creator. Now I want to argue that this world is the sort of world we would expect to exist if it were created by God.

So let's suppose that a certain sort of God does in fact exist. I am thinking of a God, like the Christian God, who creates the world and human beings and wants human beings to worship, love and obey God. But suppose God does not want to coerce them into doing so (indeed, love can hardly be coerced); instead, God wants human beings to decide *freely* and *rationally* to worship, love and obey God. Accordingly, God creates human beings as morally, spiritually and intellectually free creatures. They can either do the right thing or do the wrong thing; they can either love God or hate God. Obviously, if God creates human beings in this way, there is a genuine risk that they will go wrong. But let's say that God's central aim in creating human beings is that as many of them as possible come freely to worship, love and obey God.

Now let's ask this question: In order to achieve those ends, what sort of world would God create? I think we can see that it would have four main characteristics.

First, *it would be a coherent and rational world.* That is, events in it would be, for the most part, regular and lawlike rather than chaotic or random. In this way God would be creating a world in which human learning and science are possible, in which humans can use their God-given rational faculties to attain knowledge.

Second, *it would be a world in which the evidence for the existence of God is ambiguous.* Of course, God could have made his own existence as obvious to us as the existence of rocks and trees. God could have made his desire that we worship, love and obey him as obvious as our own desires are to us. But if God had done that, it would have resulted in a world in which we were not rationally free to say no to him. So if it is going to be possible for people freely and rationally to reject God, then God must make a world in which his existence and nature are at least somewhat hidden. God must, so to speak, hide—although, of course, not too well. It must be possible for people to find God too.

Third, *it would be a world of moral ambiguity*. That is, God must not create a world in which wrongdoing is immediately followed by punishment or virtuous acts by rewards. It must be a world in which people can sometimes do selfish and immoral deeds with impunity. If not, our moral freedom rationally to do wrong would be removed. It must also be a world in which humans must face challenges, risks, dangers and problems. Both disaster and success must be real possibilities.

We can see this point by imagining a utopian world. Let's conceive of a world in which human beings experience no pain or suffering, a world entirely plastic to our wishes. I think creating such a world would be inimical to God's purposes; God's desires for us would be thwarted. For one thing, humans in a utopian world would have little sense of what is morally right and wrong, and little feeling of obligation to do what is right. This is because our sense of what is morally wrong is closely tied to causing other people needless pain. More importantly, in a utopian world, human beings would sense no need of God—no need of divine guidance or protection or forgiveness.

Fourth, *it would be a world in which humans long for redemption and in which redemption is possible*. That is, humans would have a certain longing for God. Maybe it would be somewhat vague; certainly it would be resistible, but it would be there, almost as "a still, small voice." And God must create a world in which when humans go wrong, God makes it possible for them to be forgiven and placed on the right path.

Now the interesting point is that I seem to have been describing *this* world, the world we live in. We do live in a world that is largely regular and lawlike, in which the evidence for God is ambiguous, in which there is moral confusion and ambiguity, and in which (so I believe) redemption is possible. In other words, my argument is that our world is just the sort of world we would expect to exist if a God created it who wanted human beings freely and rationally to decide to worship, love and obey him. This fact tends to confirm the belief that the world was created by God.

## The Generic Cosmological Argument

My second argument is an actual theistic proof.[2] It is not original to me, of course; indeed it is a version of an ancient argument for the existence of God, usually called the cosmological argument.[3] Now few people who believe in God do so because of a theistic proof (and, as pointed out earlier, I do not do so). Nevertheless, even for religious people, natural theology can serve a useful purpose. If a powerful theistic proof could be produced, it might well have the effect of increasing the confidence of religious believers. That is, it could show that belief in God has a rational basis, that belief in the existence of God is not—as religious skeptics often charge—gullible, credulous or superstitious.

I will call the argument I am about to give the generic cosmological argument (GCA). Although to my knowledge nobody else presents the argument in just this way, it has strong affinities with cosmological arguments presented by Aquinas, Gottfried Wilhelm Leibniz and Samuel Clarke. Here then is the GCA:

(1) If the existence of the universe can be explained, then God exists.

(2) Everything can be explained.

(3) The universe is a thing.

(4) Therefore, the universe can be explained.

(5) Therefore God exists.

I will now clarify the argument. Three terms need definition. By the term *the universe* (or *the world*), I simply mean the sum total of everything that has ever existed or will exist (minus God, if God exists). By the term *God*, I mean some sort of divine reality or divine realities. I do not think the GCA, even if it is an entirely successful theistic proof, necessarily proves the existence of the God of Christianity—a being that is unique, all-powerful, all-knowing, loving and so on. But if the GCA is successful, it certainly does prove the existence of some sort of divine reality or necessary being (NB), which of course could possibly be the God of theism.[4] By the term *thing* I simply mean a being or entity ("substance," as some philosophers would call it)—something that has an identity distinct from other things and is a property bearer.

Second, I will briefly discuss the premises of the GCA. Premise (1) simply claims that if there is any explanation of the existence of the universe, then God must exist and provide that explanation. This premise seems perfectly sensible because if God exists, then the explanation for the existence of the universe and everything in it is just this: God created it. And this seems to be about the only sort of explanation that could be given. If no God or godlike creator of the universe exists, it seems that the universe will have no explanation whatsoever for its existence. Its existence will be what we might call a "brute fact." It is just there, and that is all that can be said.

Premise (2) is a version of a principle that philosophers call the "principle of sufficient reason" (PSR). There are many versions of the PSR; I will interpret it to mean simply this: *Everything that exists has a reason for its existence.*[5] That is, if something x exists, there must be a reason or explanation why x exists. Defenders of the PSR usually admit that the PSR cannot be proved, since it constitutes one of the basic axioms of rational thought against which all other claims or statements are measured. That is, we normally try to argue for the truth of a proposition by means of other propositions that are more evident or certain than it, but in the case of the PSR (so this argument goes), there are no propositions more certain or evident than it that can be used in this way.

But the PSR—so its defenders claim—is rationally indispensable in that it is presupposed in all rational thought. Richard Taylor says that you cannot argue for the PSR without assuming it; he calls the PSR "a presupposition of reason itself."[6] We encounter thousands of existing things every day, and we always assume that there is some reason or explanation why they exist. Suppose one day you were to encounter something unusual—a strange animal or an automobile completely unknown to you. You would dismiss as absurd any such statement as "There is no reason why it exists; it's just there—that's all." That is, your commitment to the truth of the PSR would make you reject out of hand any suggestion that the existence of the thing is entirely random or inexplicable, a brute fact. Moreover, it needs to be pointed out that there are *no* existing things about which we know that they have no explanation for their existence.

Premise (3) represents what we might call the "lumping together" strategy that we see in many versions of the CA. The typical move is to lump together all the existing things, or all the contingent things that have ever existed or will exist, and call it "reality" or "the world" or "the universe." Then causal questions are asked about this huge aggregate—questions like Who made it? or Where did it come from? or Why is it here? or What is its cause? Premise (3) simply says that the huge aggregate that we call "the universe" is itself a thing about which such causal questions can coherently be asked.

Suppose a critic of the GCA wanted to deny premise (3). If so, the response to the critic would be to point out that the universe has the two essential characteristics of "things." First, it has an identity apart from other things; the universe is not the same thing as the earth or as my computer, for example. Second, the universe is a property bearer. That is, it has certain unique properties like a certain pressure, density, temperature, space-time curvature and so on. In its very early history everything was so smashed together that there wasn't even atomic structure, so that the only contingent thing in existence was the universe itself. Accordingly, premise (3) seems highly plausible.

Premise (4) is entailed by (2) and (3). That is, if it is true, as premise (3) says, that the universe is a thing, and if it is true, as premise (2) says, that everything can be explained, then it strictly follows, as premise (4) says, that the universe can be explained. It is impossible for (2) and (3) to be true and (4) false. The conclusion of the GCA follows from (1) and (4). If it is true, as (1) says, that if the universe can be explained, then God exists, and if it is true, as (4) says, that the universe can in fact be explained, then it strictly follows, as (5) says, that God exists. Because of the argument form known as *modus ponens*, it is impossible for (1) and (4) to be true and (5) false.

Now the GCA looks at first glance to have promise as a theistic proof. But some have argued that it commits the fallacy of begging the question, and accordingly fails.[7] (Of course other objections are often raised against the CA,[8] but with one exception—an objection we will consider later in this chapter—we will focus here just on the question-begging objection.)

In order to clarify this objection to the GCA I will refer to the transcript of a famous debate in 1948 on BBC Radio. The debaters were Bertrand Russell, the famous atheist philosopher, and Frederick Copleston, SJ, the eminent historian of philosophy. The debate topic was the existence of God. In a discussion of the CA, Copleston remarked, "Well, my point is that what we call the world is intrinsically unintelligible, apart from the existence of God."[9]

Copleston thus in effect endorsed premise (1) of the GCA. But Russell consistently took the position that the world has no explanation and that it is illegitimate to ask for an explanation of the world. Russell thus in effect insisted on denying premise (2) of the GCA, which is the PSR. "I should say that the universe is there, and that's all," Russell said; "the notion of the world having an explanation is a mistake."[10]

The debate over the CA then ground to an inconclusive halt, with Russell unwilling to grant the PSR and Copleston unable to convince him of its truth. As Copleston wrote at the end of his own discussion of Aquinas's Five Ways,

> If one does not wish to embark on the path which leads to the affirmation of transcendent being, ... one has to deny the reality of the problem, assert that things "just are" and that the existential problem in question is a pseudo-problem. And if one refuses even to sit down at the chess-board and make a move, one cannot, of course, be checkmated.[11]

What the Russell-Copleston debate shows, according to some critics, is that at least some versions of the CA, doubtless including the GCA, fail as theistic proofs because they commit the fallacy of begging the question. Now there are many ways in which an argument can beg the question. At issue here is the question begging engaged in when one's argument contains a premise or premises that will only be acceptable to those who already accept the conclusion. As an illustration, notice this theistic proof:

(6) Either God exists or $7 + 5 = 13$.

(7) $7 + 5$ does not $= 13$.

(8) Therefore, God exists.[12]

This argument is certainly formally valid; it is impossible for (6) and (7) to be true and (8) false. And for theists (those who believe in the existence of God), it is also sound; that is, they hold both its premises—that is, (6) and (7)—to be true. Now nearly everybody will grant the truth of (7), and theists are happy also to grant the truth of (6). But the problem here is that no sensible person who denies or doubts the conclusion of the argument (i.e., no sensible atheist or agnostic) will grant the truth of (6). There is no reason to grant (6) apart from a prior commitment to the existence of God. Thus the (6) to (8) theistic proof is an unsuccessful theistic proof because it begs the question.

Returning to the GCA, the criticism we are discussing argues that it begs the question at the point of premise (2), "Everything can be explained" (i.e., at the point where the PSR is introduced). I explain the objection in this way: it is clear to all concerned that the GCA is formally valid; so the deepest question we can ask about it is whether its premises are true. Now premises (1) and (3) appear to be beyond reproach and can be accepted by any sensible person. But what about (2)? Well, there is a certain set of rational persons who will be much inclined to consider premise (2) true as well (i.e., inclined to accept the truth of the PSR). These people may accordingly consider the GCA to be both valid and sound (again, we are ignoring other possible objections to the GCA). That is, these folk might well consider the GCA a successful proof of the existence of God.

The people I have in mind are of course theists (i.e., people who already believe in the existence of God). Those folk quite naturally accept the suggestion that everything can be explained. They do so because they hold that the universe and everything in it (the whole of reality minus God) can be explained in some such terms as "God created it." But here is the crucial point: there is also a certain set of rational persons who will be much inclined to reject premise (2). These folk are atheists. No atheist like Bertrand Russell will have much inclination to grant the truth of premise (2). Such persons will hold that the PSR is false because there is at least one existing thing—the universe itself—that has always existed and cannot be explained. Its existence is simply a brute fact.

If the defender of the GCA can find a way of arguing convincingly for the truth of the PSR that does not appeal to or presuppose the existence of God, then the GCA might well constitute a successful theistic proof (depending of course on whether other objections to it can also be answered). In the absence of such an argument, the GCA, according to the objection we are considering, fails because it requires a premise that should not be granted by those the GCA is aimed at—namely, atheists and agnostics. Thus, since even defenders of the PSR admit that it cannot be proved, the GCA fails as a theistic proof. One of its crucial premises will only be acceptable to those who already accept its conclusion.

The point is not that only theists accept the PSR. Some atheists affirm it. The point is, as Bertrand Russell saw, that atheists *should not* affirm the PSR. In order to be consistent, they must insist that there is no explanation of why there is any reality at all as opposed to nothing. Accordingly—so the objection we are considering concludes—the GCA begs the question.

But perhaps the objection that the GCA fails as a theistic proof because it begs the question is too hasty. It seems correct to say that rational theists quite naturally accept the PSR and that rational atheists and agnostics do not, or rationally should not, do so. But does it follow that the GCA, or indeed any version of the CA that relies on the PSR, accordingly begs the question? Perhaps the answer to that question will depend on the aim, goal or purpose of the GCA.

Suppose the goal of the GCA is *to convince all atheists and agnostics to believe in the existence of God* or *to constitute an argument that rationally should convince all atheists and agnostics to believe in the existence of God.* Then, of course, the objection to the GCA that we are considering would appear to stand. The GCA would be a failure as a theistic proof. It would achieve neither purpose because rational and thoroughly convinced atheists and agnostics will reject its second premise.

But suppose the goal of the GCA is instead *to strengthen the belief of theists in the existence of God* or *to show theists that they can know that God exists.* If something like this is the purpose or goal of the GCA (which is a view I do not hold), then the objection to the GCA that we are considering appears to fail. It will not matter that atheists and agnostics rationally should reject the GCA's second premise. Since the theists at whom the argument is aimed all accept its second premise, the GCA might well (again depending on what is to be said about other objections that might be raised against it) constitute a successful proof of the existence of God.

But it seems that most theistic proofs in the history of philosophy, including the many versions of the CA that we find there, are offered with at least some sort of apologetic purpose in mind—that is, with some such goal in the mind of the theistic prover like showing to any rational person that belief in God can be rational. Theistic proofs have rarely been offered, so far as I can see, for intramural use only, for believers only. I will take it, then, that the actual aim or goal of the GCA is to *demonstrate the existence of God* and thus to *demonstrate the rationality of belief in the existence of God.* That is, what a successful theistic proof aims to do is substantiate the theist's belief in God, give a convincing reason for it, show that it is credible, show that it is *true.* But who is it to be demonstrated to? I suggest that theistic proofs aim to demonstrate the rationality of theistic belief to all rational persons (whoever exactly they are), theists *or* atheists.

One way to do this is to convince folk that the premises of the theistic proof under consideration are more plausible than their denials. The premise we are concerned with is premise (2) of the GCA:

(2) Everything can be explained.

And its denial is,

(2') It is false that everything can be explained.

Which then is more plausible: (2) or (2')? And that question, in the context of the current discussion, amounts to this: Is it possible to argue convincingly for the truth of the PSR in such a way as not to appeal to or presuppose the existence of God?[13]

It is surely possible to argue for the truth of the PSR without invoking or presupposing God. The question is whether it is possible to do so convincingly. The argument normally used by defenders of the PSR is the one briefly suggested previously—namely, that the PSR is an indispensable requirement of reason. That is, it is an intuition shared by all rational folk (except perhaps atheists and agnostics when they are objecting to the CA) about the way reality operates. It is a kind of natural belief or basic assumption that all rational people quite normally make. In this way—so defenders of the PSR say—it is not unlike the belief that

(9) My epistemic faculties do not systematically mislead me.

Clearly our faculties for gaining true beliefs about and even knowledge of the world (faculties like memory, perception, reasoning, etc.) sometimes mislead us, but any attempt to argue that they systematically mislead us would involve assuming the reliability of our epistemic faculties. So no rational person can deny (9).

The point can be made in a slightly different way: just as it is necessary for our survival as living organisms on the earth that we accept (9), so it is necessary for our survival that we accept the PSR. Imagine the life of those who seriously doubted the PSR. Such people would—so it seems—live in constant fear that no matter what precautions they took, dangerous things might always pop into existence in their vicinity uncaused—things like hungry lions or speeding trains or deep chasms or armed terrorists. Thus—so the argument concludes—human nature compels us to accept the PSR.

Is this a convincing argument? Perhaps it is to theists, who will say, "The PSR seems true to me. The arguments against it seem to me to fail, and it is rational for me to trust my faculties." But it will surely not convince the Bertrand Russells of this world. Such folk will happily grant that (9) is not rationally deniable, but they will deny that the PSR has that same status. They will happily deny that tigers, lions, chasms and terrorists pop into existence uncaused, but they will still insist on the rationality of holding the *whole* of reality (i.e., the universe itself) to be uncaused. Moreover— so they will ask—who says that the demands of human reason are all satisfied? Is reality bound to agree with our presuppositions, even presuppositions that otherwise seem rational? In short, as J. L. Mackie argues, even if it is true that reason demands that we hold that the PSR is true, that does not show that the PSR is true.[14]

Mackie is surely correct in allowing that the universe need not comply with what he calls our "intellectual preferences." I have an intellectual preference that the mathematics of quantum theory be much simpler than they in fact are. Perhaps many people share that preference. But even if I am right about what people would prefer, that shows nothing about the way reality is. However, it is a long way from this undeniable point to the claim that a conclusion that we cannot rationally deny or cannot help believing is false. If in some sense we cannot help but accept the PSR and have no good reason to think it nonetheless false, it is pointless to suggest that we take seriously the possibility that it is false.

As noted earlier, several objections are often raised against the CA besides the begging-the-question criticism we have been principally concerned with. Although I am ignoring most of them for present purposes, there is one that seems highly relevant to our discussion and should be considered. The objection is this: If GCA is a successful argument, the "god" or necessary being that it proves to exist is not the God of theism or even any lesser godlike sentient being, but rather the universe or physical matter itself. And an argument that proves the existence, or indeed the necessary existence, of the universe itself hardly does much to bolster the epistemic status of belief in God.

But it does not seem sensible to consider the universe or physical reality to be a necessary being. I cannot quite prove this by arguing that "Everything in the universe is a contingent thing; therefore the universe is a contingent thing," for that argument might well commit the fallacy of composition. Sometimes such arguments are clearly fallacious ("Every member of the human race has a mother; therefore the human race has a mother"). Although at other times they are perfectly acceptable ("All the tiles in this mosaic are blue; therefore the whole mosaic is blue"). Whether or not the inference goes through in the case of the world's contingency, it is still a meaningful fact about the universe that none of its members is necessary.

That fact strongly suggests that there is no telling reason to consider the universe a necessary being. If we knew that the universe were everlasting, that might suggest it is a necessary thing. But those who would so argue would still have to overcome the obstacle of Richard Taylor's trenchant argument to the effect that something can be both everlasting and contingent. He says: suppose, contrary to fact, that the sun and the moon are both everlasting. Then moonlight would also be everlasting but still contingent, because it would (everlastingly) depend for its existence on sunlight.[15] Moreover, we do not know that the universe—physical reality—is everlasting. Indeed, all indications are that it began at the big bang some 6.5 billion years ago (or whenever it occurred). And we have no basis whatsoever—no physics—for suggesting that anything existed before the big bang.[16]

A telling point against the objection to the GCA that we are considering is this: even if the universe were everlasting, it would still make sense to ask, Why should it exist at all? That is, why is there a cosmos or space-time reality at all? Why is there anything and not nothing? There is no absurdity at all in the idea of there being nothing at all, no universe. (No one would be there to notice that state of affairs, of course, but that does nothing to rule out the possibility.) It follows that nothing about universe implies or even suggests that it is a necessary being. Accordingly, the objection to the GCA that we are considering fails.

Where, then, have we arrived? What does our discussion imply about the epistemic status of belief in God? If the purpose of the GCA is *to demonstrate to any rational person that belief in the existence of God is rational,* then our conclusion ought to be that the GCA (assuming it emerges unscathed by other criticisms) *can* constitute a successful theistic proof. This is because defenders of the GCA, as we have seen, are perfectly capable of making a rational case for its truth that does not invoke or presuppose God. It seems that even atheists will be able to understand (though they might not agree with or be convinced by) the argument that the

PSR is a demand of rational thought. A strong case can be made—a case that any sensible person can understand—that belief in the PSR is rational.

But theists can also understand (though they might not agree with or be convinced by) the argument that while the PSR applies well to existing items like animals, automobiles and houses (things that have finite lifespans, things that come into and later pass out of existence), it does not apply to the megathing of the universe itself. Bertrand Russell might be right that it is a mistake to expect that reality itself has an explanation.

But which then is more plausible,

    (2) Everything can be explained.

or

    (2') It is false that everything can be explained?

Since, as we have seen, commitment to (2') does not entail commitment to the absurd notion that things like animals, automobiles and houses can come into existence uncaused (one can consistently hold that the universe itself is the only exception to the PSR), it does not seem possible to show which is more plausible.[17] We appear to be left with the possibility that the theist's belief in the existence of God might well be rational, given the theist's rational acceptance of (2), and that the atheist's disbelief in the existence of God might well also be rational, given the atheist's rational acceptance of (2').

But it is important to note that even this relatively irenic conclusion—that both atheists and theists can be rational—has an important consequence. If the conclusion of this chapter is correct (and again if the GCA can withstand other objections that might be raised against it), then belief in God (or some godlike being or beings who is or are responsible for the existence of the universe) is rational. Hence, it is rational to hold that naturalism and physicalism are false.

This is not a trivial conclusion. Why? Because no objection to theism is more common than the objection that in believing in God, theists are being softheaded, gullible and credulous; they are violating the ethics of belief and are setting a poor epistemic example. For example, Kai Nielsen (I could have quoted a host of others) says, "For someone living in the twentieth century with a good philosophical and a good scientific education, who thinks carefully about the matter . . . for such a person it is irrational to believe in God."[18] In the light of the GCA, this objection to theism collapses.

## Our Need of God

What keeps people from God? Obviously, some folk are either theoretical or practical atheists because they were raised that way, like I was raised to believe in God. Others have known religious believers who were cruel or dishonest or hypocritical. Others are concerned about great evils historically committed by the church— its support, for example, of anti-Semitism, the oppression of women or slavery. In academic communities one frequently encounters the assertion that intellectual difficulties constitute the main problem. The paucity of evidence for God, the lack of a convincing solution to the problem of evil or the existence of other equally plausible religions—these sorts of items are often mentioned. And there is no doubt that such factors are significant. But Christianity teaches that the deepest reason for theoretical or practical atheism is pride. People do not want to admit that they need the guidance or protection or forgiveness of God.

There is even an argument against the existence of God that I think is convincing to very many people today. Let's call it the lifestyle argument against the existence of God. It's a simple argument, a two-step proof:

> (1) I am not living and do not want to live the kind of
>     life that God would want me to live if God existed.
>
> (2) Therefore, God does not exist.

Now the lifestyle argument is obviously absurdly fallacious as a piece of logic. But that does not prevent people from being influenced by it.

Here is the main reason I hold that atheism, in either of its permutations, can be unworkable: *You might find some day that you need God.* For example, you might encounter a problem in your life that desperately needs solving and you are unable to solve it. Many people in fact come to God in the midst of crises like that. Indeed, people never come to God unless they feel a need for God in their lives.

Maybe one day you will find yourself laid off at work, with a family to support and no immediate prospects. Maybe one day you will find yourself with an alcohol or drug problem that you are no longer able to resist, one that threatens your career, your marriage, your self-respect and maybe even your life. Maybe one day you will be told that your spouse is dying of cancer, and you cannot face the prospect of life without him or her. Maybe one day you will be told that you have a dreaded disease with no known cure, and you have at most a few months to live. Maybe one day you will discover that your teenage daughter is pregnant or that your son is in trouble with the police. Maybe one day you will find that the terrible guilt you feel from some past action of yours is crushing you, and you have no idea how to get rid of it. Maybe one night you will wake up with the sickening and empty realization that your life has no purpose or meaning, that you're just treading water, that something is missing. In those sorts of situations, I say, you may discover that you need God.

In Matthew 13:44, Jesus said: "The kingdom of heaven is like a treasure hidden in a field, which someone found and hid; then in his joy he goes and sells all that he has and buys that field." We can imagine a first-century Palestinian man perhaps looking for some lost sheep after a storm. In someone else's field he finds a box half uncovered by the runoff of rainwater. He discovers that the box is full of treasure and then hurriedly covers it up. He speaks as calmly as possible with the owner of the field and establishes how much he wants for it. He then excitedly sells all his own fields and property in order to raise the purchase price of the field that contains the treasure.

Finding the help of God in the midst of a crisis in life can be one of the greatest things in the world. It is worth any amount of money. But exactly what is the treasure Jesus had in mind? This is an important question because Christianity claims to offer us something, to be sure, but not immunity or rescue from life's problems. Christians are no more cancer free or securely employed than atheists. So what exactly is so priceless?

Augustine once offered a prayer using these words: "O God, you have made us for yourself, and our hearts are restless until they repose in thee."[19] The Christian claim is that we human beings need God, and the reason we need God is, as I suggested earlier, that God created us to need God. Of course there are many things that we need in order to thrive as human beings—air to breathe, food to eat, shelter from the elements, the nurturing love of parents and the like. But the Christian claim is that the most important human need—far more basic than any of these others— is our need for loving fellowship with God. For many people the first step in finding God is confessing their inability to save themselves, to find meaning in life, to find release from guilt, to be able to continue after enduring one of life's crushing blows. Some people call Christianity a crutch. Maybe the first step in finding God is to admit that Christianity *is* a crutch, but a crutch that you need. If you have a broken leg, a crutch is a good thing.

**Finding God**

How then do you find God? Well, you must sincerely *desire* to find God. "Draw near to God, and he will draw near to you" (James 4:8). God, then, rewards those who sincerely seek God and truly want God's help. And a certain degree of faith is required. Hebrews 11:6 says, "Without faith it is impossible to please God, for whoever would approach him must believe that he exists and that he rewards those who seek him." Having this kind of faith does not come easily for many people. Fortunately, faith can grow and deepen as you sincerely try to honor God. All that God requires at the outset of a life of faith is an honest desire for his help.

The priceless thing I was speaking about is nothing other than a right relationship with God. It is priceless for two reasons. First, it satisfies our deepest need as human beings. The first responsibility of life, according to Christianity, is to know God. Thus Jesus said: "Strive first for the kingdom of God and his righteousness, and all these things [things like food, drink and clothing] will be given to you as well" (Matthew 6:33). Second, it brings with it, as a kind of serendipitous afterthought, such things as peace of mind, a sense of purpose in life, even joy. Our hearts are no longer restless when they repose in God.

# IS THE BIBLE'S PICTURE
# OF JESUS RELIABLE?

In this chapter, I will argue that the Gospels in the New Testament are reliable.[1] That is, the claims they make—preeminently their historical claims—can be trusted. I also believe that the New Testament's theological and ethical teachings are reliable, but I will not be able to say much about them.

The Bible contains discrepancies and inconsistencies that I am not able to harmonize sensibly. Accordingly, I do not hold that the Bible is inerrant, as that term is often understood.[2] But I do hold to a robust view of biblical reliability; I approach the Bible with what we might call a hermeneutic of trust. My inclination is to accept what it says unless I find convincing evidence not to do so.

I will be opposing people I call "New Testament critics," by which I mean scholars who are in my opinion unnecessarily skeptical and negative in their judgments and who consequently deny that the New Testament is historically reliable. There are two main types of New Testament critics. The first sort holds that since the New Testament is not historically reliable, that constitutes compelling reason to reject Christianity. The others think that despite the historical unreliability of the New Testament, it is still possible and even important to follow Christ. The version of Christianity that these folks accept is usually highly revisionist.

I do not suggest that the central purpose of the Evangelists (Gospel writers) was to write accurate history. I think their deepest aim is eloquently stated in John 20:31: "These [words] are written so that you [the reader] may come to believe that Jesus is the Messiah, the Son of God, and that through believing you may have life in his name."

In this essay I must be both selective in the topics that I will discuss and brief. Here is a brief road map of where we will be going. In the next section I will respond to four arguments often given by New Testament critics. Then I will offer three arguments of my own in favor of the reliability of the Gospels. Last, I will discuss some implications of what I have said.

One last preliminary point: I believe in God—that is, in an all-powerful, all-knowing and loving creator of the heavens and the earth. Moreover, I am no deist; I believe that God can and occasionally does intervene in human history to do things like rescue people from slavery, promulgate laws, inspire prophets with messages and send his Son to earth. I mention this point because some New Testament critics either do not believe in God at all or believe in God but deny that God ever intervenes. But unfortunately I do not have space to refute the claim that the New Testament must be unreliable because it records miracles.[3]

## Arguments of New Testament Critics

So I will now consider four arguments of New Testament critics.

*1. The New Testament documents are faith statements, not historical writings.* It is quite true that the books of the New Testament were written by people who wanted their readers to believe in Jesus. Their books are not neutral or unbiased. But of course that fact by itself does not entail that what they say about Jesus is false. Suppose I want to tell you about some person in hopes that you will admire her. In such a case, does it follow that the best way for me achieve this end is to exaggerate or misrepresent the facts about her? Not necessarily. I would have thought that the best way to convince people to believe in Jesus is to tell the truth about him.

Among New Testament critics, it is often assumed that if a given Gospel text seems to have a theological purpose (i.e., fits with the author's theological or apologetic stance), it does not record accurate history. But are authors who are deeply devoted to some person or idea unable to be objective about it? That hardly follows. Consider holocaust survivors: most of them are passionately committed to the moral wrongness of genocide and the survival of the Jewish people, but are extremely careful to record their experiences accurately.[4]

Moreover, in the case of Jesus, the presence during the oral period (roughly AD 30–70) of witnesses who had been with Jesus and who could correct false accounts constituted a deterrent against people simply inventing flattering items about Jesus. There is no denying that stories about Jesus were translated, edited, paraphrased and recontextualized during that period. But many New Testament critics ignore the effect of the continuing presence of eyewitnesses. It is almost as if they assume that the witnesses simply disappeared during the oral period, so that the stories were told and passed on only by anonymous communities. But, as Richard Bauckham argues, the disciples and other witnesses remained crucial during the period of oral transmission.[5]

**2. The text of the New Testament is unreliable.** It is sometimes argued that the surviving manuscripts of New Testament documents contain so many variants that they are unreliable; we cannot be sure what the originals said.[6] But this claim is exaggerated. There certainly are variant readings in the manuscripts. Most are due to unintentional errors of copyists; they concern spelling, word order, minor grammatical differences, repeating a word or skipping a line. Such errors can easily be corrected. Some changes were intentionally made by copyists, but even in those cases we can usually see what the scribe had in mind (e.g., to bring the text into conformity with other biblical texts or with accepted doctrine) and can fix the error.

There are admittedly a few cases where it is difficult to decide what the original text said. Do any of them concern issues that are important for Christians? Sure. I suppose it is important to know whether Christians will be protected if they handle rattlesnakes or drink poison. But this issue can be settled easily: text critics agreed long ago that Mark 16:9-20 is a later addition. Is the Trinity important to Christians? Certainly. So should it bother Christians that the trinitarian benediction in 1 John 5:7-8 was probably added later? Not at all: Christians believe in the Trinity on other grounds. The story of the woman taken in adultery (John 7:53–8:11) is an important pericope, beloved of Christians. But it does not appear in the earliest texts of the Fourth Gospel. Indeed, it reads more like a text from the Synoptic Gospels (which is possibly the reason some manuscripts place it in Luke). Does it nevertheless record an actual event? Yes, that is quite possible.

So, yes, some of the textual variants do concern important matters. But the point is that the problems they raise can be solved and have been accounted for long ago by those who believe that the New Testament is reliable. In the vast majority of cases, text critics agree on, and Christians can know, what the original texts said. Very few difficult variants raise any serious questions about the text's meaning. We possess a text of the Greek New

Testament that is accurate enough to be more than adequate for religious and theological purposes.

***3. The New Testament documents are late.*** It is true that the Gospels were written some years after the events they record. Jesus was probably crucified in AD 29 or 30. The earliest New Testament books—some of the Pauline Epistles—were probably written just over twenty years later. Mark was probably written some time between AD 65 and 70. Matthew and Luke were probably written some ten to fifteen years after Mark. And John, the last canonical Gospel, was probably written in the early 90s.

In general the closer in time witnesses or historians are to the events they speak or write about the better. But some New Testament critics accordingly hold that what we encounter in the Gospels is not Jesus himself (i.e., the actual events as they occurred in, say, AD 29) but the church's understanding of Jesus in the 80s or 90s, when those books were receiving final form. Thus—so it is concluded—many of the events recorded in those books did not occur as described.

Is this true? Well, in the Gospels we certainly do come in contact with the consciousness of the Evangelists at the time they were written. But that fact does not rule out the possibility that we also come in contact with Jesus himself, with events that occurred in AD 29 or 30. Indeed, in reading the work of any historian writing about any person or period in history, we do naturally come in contact with the consciousness of the historian at the time the work was written. But if the historian has done a worthwhile job of writing history, we also come in contact with the person or events written about. I believe that in the Gospels—despite the fact that they are written years afterward from the perspective of faith—we can learn much of what Jesus said and did.

When it comes to constructing "a life of Jesus," New Testament critics disagree with each other. Writing revisionist books about Jesus seems to be a cottage industry these days.[7] Was Jesus essentially an apocalyptic prophet, a teacher of wisdom, a healer, a cynic philosopher or perhaps a magician? All such notions have been defended. Nevertheless, a rough consensus emerges in such circles on what we can know about the life of Jesus. Here are the main points: he was a Palestinian Jew from Nazareth who was baptized by John the Baptist and became a public figure in first-century Palestine; he selected a group of disciples and engaged in a ministry of preaching, teaching and healing; under the influence of Jewish apocalyptic thinking he preached the kingdom of God and came into conflict with Jewish groups such as the Pharisees and Sadducees; although he ministered mainly in Galilee, he eventually came to Jerusalem, where he was arrested, tried and crucified.[8]

I certainly accept that these are facts; my difficulty is seeing how anybody could suppose that this is *all* or almost all that we can know about Jesus. Are these minimum facts sufficient to explain the existence of the Christian church and the traditions about Jesus in the New Testament? For example, why would anybody suggest that this relatively innocuous figure was God incarnate? Aren't scholars rationally obliged to posit a "life of Jesus" that would help explain why the church so quickly arrived at notions like Jesus' sinlessness, preexistence, divine Sonship and unity with the Father? Surely a great deal more than this needs to be said about Jesus.[9]

Since many New Testament critics deny that Jesus was divine, there is intense speculation about the sources of and influences on New Testament Christology. Some suggest that notions like preexistence and divinity were arrived at after a long and complicated quasi-evolutionary process involving embellishments in the Jesus tradition due to religious experiences, social conditions in the Christian community or the influence of other cultures and religions. A mere Jewish prophetic teacher eventually became a preexistent being, ontologically one with God.

Two points need to be made here. First, those who argue for some such scenario have not made a compelling case. Despite efforts to find pre-Christian parallels to and influences on New Testament Christology, no assured parallels and influences have been found. Moreover, the very idea of extensive pagan influences on pre-Pauline Christology, which some New Testament critics have suggested, seems to me implausible. Second, nowhere in the New Testament, or in any of the sources or layers of tradition that supposedly antedate and influence it, has anybody located a purely human Jesus. Scholars such as C. F. D. Moule, Martin Hengel, N. T. Wright and Larry Hurtado have argued that even the most elevated Christological notions are very old indeed.[10] Some of the highest Christological notions are found, either explicitly or by implication, in the letters of Paul, the earliest datable documents in the New Testament.

Of course, even if divinity claims are early, that does not show that they are true. I have only been arguing against the idea that the New Testament's high claims for Jesus are late and unreliable embellishments.

*4. The New Testament documents are contradictory.* I do not deny that there are different emphases and discrepancies in the New Testament. Many of the apparent inconsistencies can be easily harmonized, and most of the intractable ones are unimportant. Still, they are there. Yet I believe there is an amazing unity to the New Testament's picture of Jesus.

But some New Testament critics reject this last claim. Dismissing an almost a priori assumption of New Testament unity in the biblical theology movement in the mid-twentieth century, many New Testament critics go overboard in the other direction. Contradictions in the New Testament are sought out with inquisitorial zeal; any attempt to harmonize two apparently discrepant passages is rejected as laughably unscholarly, and it seems to be assumed that there is no such thing as "the New Testament view" of this or that. The New Testament is not a coherent book but a kind of awkward and uneven anthology. Accordingly, New Testament critics often insist that there are many Christologies in the New Testament. That is, the New Testament contains many competing and mutually inconsistent interpretations of Jesus; harmonization of them is impossible. Accordingly, no one biblical Christology is normative for all Christians.

Again, some of this is correct. There *are* different Christological emphases in various New Testament texts, and facile harmonization must be avoided because it can cause us to miss the great richness and variety of New Testament Christology. Nevertheless, I insist that harmonization of apparently discrepant texts is a natural and rational impulse, whether in biblical criticism or ordinary life. All historians at times try to reconcile apparently discrepant testimony.

And the different interpretations of Jesus are best seen as related insights that developed among different persons and communities over time. I believe these interpretations are mutually consistent and are best expressed in terms of the church's classical doctrine of the incarnation. It is a telling fact that theologians from the second century onward (e.g., Ignatius) were sufficiently impressed by the unity of the New Testament pictures of Jesus to claim that they can be synthesized in the notion of incarnation. So it seems to me that there does exist what we can call a "New Testament picture of Jesus." Despite differences of emphasis, all the New Testament writers agree on crucial points.[11]

## The Reliability of the Gospels

Now I will offer three arguments in favor of the reliability of the picture of Jesus in the Gospels.[12]

*1. Paul on Jesus.* Scholars sometimes say that the apostle Paul knew or cared little about the life of Jesus. But that is not true. True, Paul never wrote a Gospel. His extant epistles were all occasional pieces that respond to various needs he saw in the individuals and churches he wrote to.

But the life and teachings of the Lord were important to Paul. This fact is easy to establish. He emphasized the need for believers to obey and even imitate Jesus (1 Corinthians 11:1; 4:10-12; 1 Thessalonians 1:6). And it is not clear how that could be done or even attempted without at least some knowledge of Jesus' life. Moreover, Paul made a careful distinction between Jesus' teachings and his own teachings (1 Corinthians 7:7-16; cf. 2 Corinthians 11:17; 1 Thessalonians 4:2, 15). Again, how could Paul do that without knowing what Jesus' teachings were?

Moreover, in broad outline we can piece together a credible "life of Jesus" by noting scattered references in the seven letters that most New Testament scholars accept as authentically Pauline (Romans, 1–2 Corinthians, Galatians, Philippians, 1 Thessalonians, Philemon). And when we compile Paul's "life of Jesus," we find that to a great extent it confirms what we find in Mark, the earliest of the Gospels, and denies virtually nothing found there.

Here is what we can find. His name was Jesus (1 Corinthians 1:1); he was a man (Romans 5:15) born of a woman (Galatians 4:4); he was Jewish, a descendant of Abraham (Galatians 3:16; 4:4) and David (Romans 1:3); he had brothers (1 Corinthians 9:5). He was sent by God to take on human form (Romans 8:3; Philippians 2:6-11); he was poor (2 Corinthians 8:9) and humble (Philippians 2:6-11); he suffered (Romans 8:17); he was loving and compassionate (Philippians 1:8); and he lived an exemplary life (Romans 15:3, 8; 2 Corinthians 8:9; Philippians 2:6-8).

Jesus gathered disciples, including Cephas and John (Galatians 1:19; 2:9), and taught people on various religious topics (1 Thessalonians 4:2), including marriage and divorce (1 Corinthians 7:10), how those who preach the gospel should make their living (1 Corinthians 9:14), blessing those who persecute you (Romans 12:14), repaying no one evil for evil (Romans 12:17), accepting all foods as clean (Romans 14:14), and his own ultimate triumphal return (1 Thessalonians 4:15-17). On the night Jesus was betrayed he took bread, broke it, gave thanks and said, "This is my body that is for you. Do this in remembrance of me." Then he took a cup and said, "This cup is the new covenant in my blood. Do this, as often as you drink it, in remembrance of me" (1 Corinthians 11:23-26).

Jesus was betrayed (1 Corinthians 11:23), was crucified by "the Jews" (1 Corinthians 1:23; 2:2; 1 Thessalonians 2:14) and was buried (1 Corinthians 15:4). On the third day (1 Corinthians 15:4) God raised him from the dead (Romans 1:4; 4:25; 6:4; 8:34; 1 Corinthians 15:4; 2 Corinthians 4:14; Galatians 1:1; 1 Thessalonians 4:14). He appeared to Peter, to "the twelve," to more than five hundred people, to James and then to all the apostles (1 Corinthians 15:5-7). Finally, as the Gospel writers do, Paul insisted that Jesus would return (1 Thessalonians 4:16-17) to be revealed (1 Corinthians 1:7) and to judge all people (Romans 2:16). Indeed, this last point constitutes a major theological innovation shared by Mark and Paul: the idea of a suffering Messiah who dies on a cross and will one day return in victory over his enemies.[13]

The importance of this point about agreement with Paul is clear: the authentically Pauline letters were all written well before Mark, and indeed within twenty to thirty years of the death of

Jesus. Accordingly, what Paul said about the life of Jesus is much more likely to be reliable on purely historical-critical grounds than something written much later. And this reliability confirms the accuracy of later texts like Mark that largely agree with Paul on the life of Jesus. Mark does not appear to be myth or fable or fiction. What we have here, then, is an impressive reason for regarding Mark as reliable.

**2. Jesus' view of himself.** A second way of approaching the question of the reliability of the picture of Jesus in the Gospels is to ask, What did Jesus think of himself?[14] The traditional way of answering this question was simply to quote Christological statements from the Fourth Gospel (e.g., "The Father and I are one" [John 10:30] or "Whoever has seen me has seen the Father" [John 14:9]). But many biblical scholars deny that these words constitute the *ipsissima verba* (the very words) of Jesus. Such statements—so they say—tell us more about the faith of the early church at the time John was written than they do about the actual teachings of Jesus.

Is that true? Well, as noted, the Gospels are not neutral, facts-only biographies of Jesus. And John's Gospel was the last canonical Gospel written and so was the furthest removed from the events it describes. As the early church recognized, it is a more overtly theological interpretation of Jesus than are the Synoptics. Moreover, since Jesus spoke and taught in Aramaic, and since the New Testament was written in Greek, then almost none of the sayings attributed to Jesus in the Gospels constitute his *ipsissima verba*.

Still, I believe that much of the material in the Gospels that implies a high Christology can in some form be traced back to Jesus. That is, despite what New Testament critics say, Jesus implicitly claimed the high status that the church attributed to him; he viewed himself as more than a prophet, as more even than the Messiah and as more than a "son of God" (where that term describes kings and other special men). He was, I believe, in some robust sense, conscious of himself as having a special and unique relation to God.

Jesus' lofty view of his own aims and vocation best explains why he was crucified. And on some theories of Jesus it is not easy to see why anybody would want to kill him. This seems to be a problem for the countercultural Jesus of the Jesus Seminar, who produces arresting and pithy religious aphorisms. People might well have taken such a Jesus as an eccentric, but hardly as the kind of person who must be killed.

Moreover, the view of Jesus found in the New Testament does a better job than revisionist views in explaining the rise of the church. It is obvious that there was a phenomenon called first-century Judaism. There was also a phenomenon called first-century Christianity. The question is, How did we get from one to the other? What explains the existence of the Christian movement? On some contemporary views of Jesus, this constitutes a difficulty. But if Jesus really performed miracles, claimed (implicitly) to be the Messiah and to have a unique and special relationship with God, and was raised from the dead, an explanation is nearby. In other words, the Gospels do a better job of explaining known facts than revisionist theories do.

Consider what Jesus did. He took it upon himself to overrule standard interpretations of the Torah, to offer forgiveness of sins,[15] to claim that his words would endure forever, to claim that the eternal destiny of persons depended on their response to him and his ministry, and to promise to be with his followers forever. He allowed them to worship him and encouraged them to pray in his name. (This same sort of high Christological strand is present even in earlier texts such as Philippians 2:5-11 and 1 Corinthians 8:6, as well as, a bit later, Colossians 1:15-20.)

So the argument is that the best explanation of early Christian worship of Jesus and lofty claims about Jesus is that Jesus himself was at least implicitly conscious of having a unique and intimate relationship with God and communicated his awareness of his own vocation and status to his followers.[16] His sense of ministry and identity was doubtless shaped by various events in his life, including the baptism, temptation, transfiguration and passion.[17]

I am not saying that any validation of Jesus' high status must rest solely, or even mainly, on what Jesus himself (explicitly or implicitly) claimed to be. Also playing crucial roles in the church's confession of Jesus as divine Lord and Son of God were the post-Easter responses to Jesus' death and resurrection and the coming of the Holy Spirit.

**3. The resurrection of Jesus.** One crucial New Testament claim about Jesus is that God raised him from the dead.[18] New Testament critics usually deny that claim; in many cases this is because they do not believe in an intervening God. But theologically orthodox scholars have made a powerful case in recent years in favor of the reality of Jesus' resurrection—indeed, in favor of his bodily resurrection.[19]

Let us define briefly two worldviews. (1) *Naturalism* is the view that the physical world exhausts reality. There are no nonphysical things like God or gods, and no violations of natural laws. Accordingly, every event that occurs can in principle be explained by methods similar to those used in the natural sciences. (2) *Supernaturalism* is the view that the physical world exists because it was brought into being, along with its natural laws, by God. And God has the ability to violate natural laws. Accordingly, not every event can be explained scientifically. My point is that once it is established that belief in supernaturalism is a defensible position (and I believe Christian philosophers have done that very thing), a strong case can be made for the resurrection of Jesus.[20]

The earliest Christians unanimously and passionately believed that Jesus was alive. Their belief in his resurrection accounts for their transformation from frightened cowards, huddling away in hiding right after the crucifixion, to courageous preachers of their Lord shortly thereafter. What this point establishes is that the earliest Christians truly *believed* that God had raised Jesus. It does not establish the truth of their belief. But it does go a long way toward refuting reductive theories of their belief—for example, what the disciples really meant is that the work of Jesus goes on or that Jesus was in some spiritual sense still present to them.

The disciples' belief in the resurrection sustained the Jesus movement and allowed it to survive and thrive. It enabled them to overcome both the discouragement they felt immediately after their leader's death and their later persecution. Moreover, criticisms of the empty tomb and appearance traditions can, in my opinion, be answered.[21] Notice that there are certain facts about the resurrection that almost no one disputes: (1) Jesus was crucified and died; (2) first-century Jews did not believe in a suffering and dying messiah; (3) first-century Jews did not believe in any kind of pre-end-time resurrection of individuals; (4) the earliest Christians believed that the tomb was empty, that the risen Jesus had appeared to several of them and that these events occurred because God had raised Jesus from the dead.

The point is that resurrection deniers face one big embarrassment: no one has ever produced a plausible naturalistic explanation of what happened after the crucifixion that accounts for these accepted facts. None of the suggested explanations—wrong tomb, swoon, hallucination, mistaken identity, myth—have any compelling evidence in their favor. Many are so weak that they collapse of their own weight once they are spelled out.[22]

Accordingly, the claim that Jesus really was raised from the dead is the best explanation of the evidence, at least for supernaturalists. I do not say that if I am correct on this point, all of Jesus' words and deeds described in the Gospels have been authenticated. But if I am indeed correct, that does impressively buttress the claim that the Gospels are reliable.

## The Religious Authority of the New Testament

I have been arguing that the Gospels are historically reliable. But why is this important? Aren't the theological and ethical teachings of Christianity more important than its historical assertions? Well, perhaps they are. And it is true that many of the teachings of Jesus do not need any historical basis for them to be wise, incisive and helpful. But some absolutely bedrock Christian claims *do* need a historical basis. Now some New Testament critics argue that the *meaning* of the resurrection (which they always explain in ways that do not involve the dead Jesus actually living again) is more important than the *historical claim* that Jesus was raised. But I would respond that if Jesus was not actually raised by God, then "the resurrection of Jesus" ultimately means virtually nothing, apart perhaps from some lessons about facing death bravely.

How can a book like the New Testament—with historical discrepancies, textual variants and differences of emphasis on theological themes—be considered religiously authoritative? Those are questions New Testament critics often pose.

My answer is this: I believe that God superintended the writing of the texts that comprise what Christians call the Bible. But that was not enough. It seems that in order for the Bible to accomplish God's purposes, God would have to (1) ensure the protection and preservation of God's basic message to humankind (e.g., by putting it into a text); (2) superintend the process of compiling that book (including deciding on the canon of that text); (3) ensure that this text could be properly interpreted (e.g., by creating a tradition of interpretation like "the rule of faith");[23] and (4) ensure its authoritative interpretation and application by creating an institution (the church) designed to do that very thing. And I believe God did all four.

There are places in the Bible where many Christians find it difficult to hear God's voice. The Bible is a human as well as divine product; there are peaks and valleys, highs and lows. What is needed, especially in the light of the murkier nooks and crannies of the Bible (among which I would include the command to slaughter all the Canaanites [e.g., Deuteronomy 2:31-35], as well as the conclusion of Psalm 137), is what I will call *theological exegesis*. This is exegesis in the light of the rule of faith. Any given text must be interpreted in the light of the Christian community's vision of the witness of the entirety of Scripture. We must always view such a vision as fallible and amendable by further exegesis. Otherwise, the freedom of the Holy Spirit to speak to us in Scripture can be curtailed. But the church's overall vision of the macromeaning of the Bible can be seen as a canon against which to test various interpretations of texts.

Three hermeneutical principles—principles that have been implicitly recognized since the church fathers—help clarify (although they do not exhaust) what I mean by theological exegesis: (1) the Old Testament is to be interpreted in terms of the New Testament, (2) obscure passages are to be interpreted in terms of clear passages and (3) everything is to be interpreted Christologically. The four Gospels, certain of the Pauline letters (notably Romans and Galatians), and many of the Psalms are to be taken as hermeneutically foundational.[24] Are they more inspired or more truly God's Word than the others? No. The claim is merely that they are more hermeneutically foundational to Christian belief and practice.

Let me illustrate. There exists in my hometown a progressive theological seminary called the Claremont School of Theology. One day several years ago I was speaking with a student I knew reasonably well, a young man who identified strongly with the gay community and was wrestling with questions about the believability of the Bible. He said that the main reason he could not accept anything like my own high view of biblical authority is, as he put it, "the Bible teaches the subjugation of women." I replied that the Bible teaches that idea only if we take all the texts in the Bible, line them up and treat them as being on a hermeneutical and theological par. But if we were to follow that procedure, we would also have to say that the Bible teaches that we should kill our disobedient sons by stoning (Deuteronomy 21:18-21) and that we should never plant our fields with two different kinds of grain (Leviticus 19:19). I said that just as Christians regard those last two commands as superseded by later and more hermeneutically foundational texts, so we should regard those texts that seem to teach the subjugation of woman. Properly interpreted—so I told him—the Bible does not teach the subjugation of women.

The opinion that the New Testament is reliable depends on a certain view of its character. It is not just that Christians *take the New Testament to be* authoritative Scripture (although we do). (As if we could also take *The Iliad* or *The Republic* or maybe even *The Critique of Pure Reason* to be Scripture if we chose to do so.) The opinion depends on the view that the New Testament is a book unlike other books, a book in which in some robust sense *God speaks to us.* Those who hold that the New Testament is reliable cannot regard it as merely or simply a human product like the works of Homer or Plato or Kant. They hold it to be, when properly interpreted, the Word of God.

As noted, I do not espouse biblical inerrancy. But I do affirm that the Bible is infallible, where I understand this to mean something like "does not mislead us in matters that are crucially related to Christian faith and practice."[25] So those who hold that the New Testament is reliable distance themselves from any notion that the New Testament is just another book like all the others. They approach the New Testament with a hermeneutic of trust. They take it to be the source of religious truth above all other sources, the norm or guide to religious truth above all norms or guides. All others are subordinate to Scripture and are to be tested by Scripture.

My arguments in this chapter do not amount to a proof that the Gospels are historically reliable. There are many New Testament reliability issues that I have not addressed. Moreover, all history deals with probabilities. But in many cases historical probabilities can be high. I believe my arguments do show that there is a strong probability that the Gospels are reliable.[26]

# WAS JESUS RAISED FROM THE DEAD?

Two of the most important theological claims of Christianity are (1) that Jesus was the incarnate Son of God, and (2) that God raised Jesus from the dead. In this chapter I want to argue in more detail than in chapter three in favor of the resurrection of Jesus. I will argue from reason and evidence alone, not from authority. That is, I will not claim that you should believe that Jesus was raised just because the Bible says so, because the pope says so or because your grandmother told you so.

The simple claim I will consider is "God raised Jesus from the dead." The case I will make will necessarily be somewhat quick and brief.[1]

## Assumptions and Definitions

My argument is based on certain assumptions. The first is that God exists. That is, I will presuppose the existence of an all-powerful, all-knowing and perfectly good creator of the heavens and the earth. Second, I will make certain assumptions about the meaning of the term *resurrection*. (1) A resurrection is a *miraculous event* brought about by God; people do not naturally rise from the dead (as opposed to the way we naturally recover from a head cold or the flu). Resurrections only happen if and when God causes them to happen. (2) Resurrection is *bodily* resurrection. The Christian claim that Jesus was (and we will be) raised is not the doctrine known as the immortality of the soul, where after death our bodies disintegrate permanently but our immaterial souls go on existing in some sort of immaterial world. And (3) resurrection is not *resuscitation*. Resuscitations occasionally occur in hospitals these days. This is when a person who has passed through certain of the stages of death (e.g., no heartbeat or breathing for several minutes) is by heroic medical measures brought back to life. And certain (what surely were) resuscitations are described in the Bible too (e.g., the raising of Lazarus). The difference is this: in resuscitations, the revived persons are restored to their old lives and will certainly die again at some later point, and that second-time death will presumably be for good. A resurrected person is raised to a new and exalted state of life and will never die again.

Let me define the word *worldview*. A worldview is a set of fundamental beliefs about how the world is. Everybody has a worldview. It is like a pair of glasses or spectacles through which you see the world and that allows you to interpret what you see. I will reintroduce two worldviews that we looked at briefly in chapter three.

*Naturalism* is a worldview that says (1) physical matter is all that exists; there are no nonphysical things like souls or spirits or gods or God; (2) no natural laws (e.g., gravity, entropy, thermodynamics) are ever violated; and accordingly (3) everything that ever occurs can in principle be explained by methods similar to those that are used in the natural sciences. There are no miracles or permanent anomalies or mysteries. Perhaps there are some phenomena that we cannot now explain, but that is because we do not now know enough about the world or about its natural laws.

*Supernaturalism* is a worldview that says (1) the physical world exists only because God brought it into existence; (2) the world does exhibit certain natural laws, but they only hold because God established them; (3) God has the ability and perhaps occasionally the intention to bring about events that otherwise (i.e., apart from God's intention) would not have occurred; and (4) accordingly, not all events can in principle be naturalistically explained. Some events can only be explained via the action of God.

Such events can be called miracles. According to Christians, the resurrection of Jesus is one such event. Accordingly, rational belief in the resurrection of Jesus presupposes supernaturalism.

## Evidence: The Empty Tomb

The Christian church has always recognized two main sources of evidence in favor of resurrection: (1) the claim that sometime soon after the death of Jesus, the tomb he had been buried in was found to be empty; and (2) the claim that sometime soon after the death of Jesus he appeared to certain people. Let us now consider these two bits of evidence in turn.

The empty tomb has broad support in the New Testament. It is mentioned in all four Gospels and is alluded to elsewhere. Mark was the earliest of the Gospels to be written. Here is Mark's account:

> When the sabbath was over, Mary Magdalene, and Mary the mother of James, and Salome bought spices, so that they might go and anoint him. And very early on the first day of the week, when the sun had risen, they went to the tomb. They had been saying to one another, "Who will roll away the stone for us from the entrance to the tomb?" When they

looked up they saw that the stone, which was very large, had already been rolled back. As they entered the tomb, they saw a young man, dressed in a white robe, sitting on the right side; and they were alarmed. But he said to them, "Do not be alarmed; you are looking for Jesus of Nazareth, who was crucified. He has been raised; he is not here. Look, there is the place they laid him. But go, tell his disciples and Peter that he is going ahead of you to Galilee; there you will see him, just as he told you." So they went out and fled from the tomb, for terror and amazement had seized them; and they said nothing to anyone, for they were afraid. (Mark 16:1-8)

Of course those who deny the resurrection of Jesus raise arguments against the empty tomb. The main criticism is that the story is late and apologetically motivated. Let's consider the lateness point first. Jesus was crucified in about AD 29 or 30. Mark, the Gospel just quoted, was probably written around AD 70, some forty years after the events it describes. Luke and Matthew were probably written in the 80s, and John, the last of the four canonical Gospels, in the 90s. But some of Paul's writings were written in the early 50s, just a few years after the crucifixion, and the criticism is that there are no explicit references to the empty tomb in those early letters. The argument then is that the empty tomb stories appeared late in the New Testament period (i.e., were invented later).

But this is misleading. There is an implicit reference to the empty tomb in 1 Corinthians, which was written in the early 50s, where Paul says of Jesus that he was crucified "and that he was buried" (1 Corinthians 15:4). And Paul, along with most first-century Jews, would surely have believed that resurrection *entailed* the empty tomb. The idea that people could be raised from the dead while their bodies remained in the tomb is a modern invention.

Moreover, although the book of Acts was written in the 80s, it records several early sermons of the disciples that were preached in Jerusalem soon after the resurrection. What we find in Acts may not of course amount to verbatim quotations of those sermons, but the basic themes in them probably do go back to early times. And it is important to note that in his sermon in Acts 2 Peter contrasts Jesus with King David. David, he said, "both died and was buried, and his tomb is with us to this day" (Acts 2:29), but the flesh of Jesus did not "experience corruption" because God raised him from the dead (Acts 2:31-32). Accordingly, it is very doubtful that the empty tomb tradition was absent in the early days of the church and only appeared later.

Now the word *apologize* to us means saying you're sorry for something you've said or done, but the Greek word *apologia* means "defense." The criticism here is that the empty tomb tradition was invented by the church as a way of defending or buttressing the claim that Jesus had been raised. But although early Christians doubtless later used the fact of the empty tomb apologetically, at first the emptiness of the tomb only caused puzzlement and consternation. It was not apologetic at all. Thus the male disciples dismissed the report of the women: "But these words seemed to them an idle tale, and they did not believe them" (Luke 24:11; see also Luke 24:22-24).

Moreover, it must be emphasized that the preaching of the resurrection of Jesus by the earliest church would have been impossible without safe evidence of an empty tomb. And the earliest recorded Jewish criticism of the resurrection—the claim that the disciples stole the body (Matthew 28:11-15)—simply presupposed the emptiness of the tomb. Apparently nobody then doubted it. It is hard to know how much time passed between the crucifixion of Jesus and the preaching of the resurrection by his disciples; Luke in Acts does not precisely tell us. But one gets the impression that it is a matter of days or at most weeks. But clearly at some point soon after the crucifixion, Jerusalem was seething with Christian preaching. People were being converted. The Jewish leaders were alarmed. If the tomb was not empty, all that the enemies of the Christian movement had to do to squelch that movement was to wheel the body of Jesus on a gurney into the place where the preaching was going on. Obviously, they did not do so. Christians say that they did not do that because they could not do it: the tomb was empty.

Moreover, if the story of the empty tomb was an apologetic device invented by the early Christians, it is bad apologetics. A made-up story, invented to defend the claim that Jesus was raised, would never have included women as the primary witnesses. As everyone knows, women in first-century Judaism did not have much respect or legal status. As Jewish historian Josephus says, they were not considered credible witnesses and were allowed to testify in court only very rarely; their testimony had to be corroborated by a man.[2] Even more striking is the figure of Mary Magdalene, "from whom seven demons had gone out" (Luke 8:2), as the principal discoverer of the empty tomb. An invented story, made as convincing and airtight as possible, would never have used such a dubious woman; it would surely have had men as the discoverers of the empty tomb.

Accordingly, the case for the empty tomb looks strong.

### Evidence: The Appearances

The second evidence of the resurrection of Jesus is the claim that soon after the resurrection Jesus appeared at various times to various individuals and groups. In his first letter to the Christians in Corinth, Paul lists the appearances as follows:

> For I handed on to you as of first importance what I in turn
> had received: that Christ died for our sins in accordance with
> the scriptures, and that he was buried, and that he was raised
> on the third day in accordance with the scriptures, and that
> he appeared to Cephas, then to the twelve. Then he appeared
> to more than five hundred brothers and sisters at one time,
> most of whom are still alive, though some have died. Then he
> appeared to James, then to all the apostles. Last of all, as to
> one untimely born, he appeared also to me.
> (1 Corinthians 15:3-8)

And here is a description of one of the appearances:

> While they were talking about this, Jesus himself stood
> among them and said to them, "Peace be with you." They
> were startled and terrified, and thought that they were seeing
> a ghost. He said to them, "why are you frightened, and why
> do doubts arise in your hearts? Look at my hands and my
> feet: see that it is I myself. Touch me and see; for a ghost
> does not have fresh and bones as you see that I have." And
> when he had said this, he showed them his hands and his
> feet. While in their joy they were disbelieving and still
> wondering, he said to them, "Have you anything here to eat?"
> They gave him a piece of broiled fish, and he took it and ate
> in their presence. (Luke 24:36-43)

As before, various criticisms have been raised against the
appearance stories. I will discuss four of them.

First, some critics claim that the resurrection accounts in the
New Testament are legends that grew over time. And of course in
the ancient world there were several accounts of raisings from the
dead of various heroes, religious figures and gods, which most of
us now consider legends. Moreover, the mention of earthquakes,
darkness at noon and angels in the New Testament accounts seem

to some critics like the kinds of spectacular miraculous flourishes that ancient legendary stories often have.

It is true that legends grow and expand with the passage of time, but so do stories based on historical kernels of truth. Think of additions that have been made to the life stories of real historical figures like King Arthur, George Washington and Abraham Lincoln. Think of additions that have been made over time to real historical events like the Trojan War, the siege of Masada or the battle of Agincourt. So the fact that additions are made to an original story does not entail that it is false.

Moreover, there simply was not enough time for legends to develop. As noted, Paul wrote some twenty years after the crucifixion when there were certainly people still alive who had experienced some of the appearances (he says as much in 1 Corinthians 15:6). And his reference in 1 Corinthians 15:3 (cited earlier) to "what I in turn had received" is a technical first-century reference to the handing on of tradition. It doubtless refers to what he had been taught about Jesus and the resurrection by the Christians who received him in Damascus soon after his conversion (or perhaps to what the Jerusalem believers told him when he visited there in AD 36 [Galatians 1:18]). Legends take many years to develop, but within weeks or even days of the crucifixion the earliest Christians were claiming that Jesus had appeared to them.

Second, some critics suggest that the "appearances" of Jesus were visions or hallucinations. But the resurrection appearances do not look like likely cases of hallucination. Jesus' followers were not expecting or even hoping for a resurrection. Many people, at different times and in scattered locations, saw the risen Jesus (is there any such thing as a group hallucination?). Some doubted that it was Jesus, and some only recognized him with difficulty. There were no drugs, high fever, or lack of food or water mentioned.

And hallucinations rarely produce longstanding convictions or radical lifestyle changes. But belief in the resurrection of Jesus did both. Hallucination looks to be an extremely improbable explanation of the appearances.

Third, some critics argue that eyewitness testimony is notoriously unreliable; experiments in social psychology have shown as much. This is true, but does it amount to a convincing argument against the appearance stories in the New Testament? I do not think so. Eyewitness testimony tends to be unreliable on various details, not on essential facts. Suppose I arranged an experiment in which five men rushed into my classroom, shouting, carrying signs and pulling me out the door. If we were later to interrogate each student who was present, we would surely find divergent memories of things like what the intruders were shouting, what their signs said, what color shirts they were wearing, maybe even precisely how many of them there were. But we would not find any students who thought that what they had just witnessed was a basketball game, a prayer meeting, a dormitory bull session or the awarding of an honorary doctorate. They would agree on the essential facts. So it is with the resurrection of Jesus. The alleged eyewitnesses were clear on the fact that they had encountered the risen Jesus.

Fourth, some critics argue that inconsistencies and discrepancies in different biblical accounts of the same appearance render them unreliable. And there surely are discrepancies in the stories. For example, how many appearances of Jesus were there in all? That is not easy to say; possibly there were seven or eight, depending on how you count. Did the women arrive at the tomb while it was still dark or after the sun had risen? At the tomb, did they encounter one young man (or angel) or two? The discrepancies undoubtedly arose over time in the oral transmission of the stories from several sources before they were written down.

Most of the discrepancies are quite easy to harmonize (e.g., "young man dressed in white" was a way of referring to an angel), a few can be harmonized with some effort, and one or two seem fairly intractable. But tellingly the accounts all agree on this point: *early on the first day of the week, certain women, notably Mary Magdalene, went to the tomb, found it empty, met an angel or angels, and were either told or else discovered that Jesus was alive.* There also is striking agreement between John's Gospel and one or more of the Synoptic Gospels (i.e., Matthew, Mark and Luke) that *the women informed Peter or other disciples of their discovery, Peter went to the tomb and found it empty, and the risen Jesus appeared to the women and gave them instructions for the disciples.* And the appearance stories in the Gospels all agree that *the risen Jesus appeared to his followers in bodily form and spoke to them.*

Moreover, even the discrepancies themselves testify in a sort of backhanded way to the truth of the basic point. They show that the Christian claim was not a made-up story, memorized and repeated verbatim by the early witnesses, like an alibi story that criminals might invent. The New Testament claim that Jesus was alive and had appeared to certain people clearly came from different believers or communities of believers and was written down at different times. That is evidence of the truth of what they say.

It should also be pointed out that the empty tomb and the appearances must stand together. Without both, the Christian claim that God raised Jesus from the dead would have collapsed in the first century. Without the appearances, the empty tomb could have been dismissed as a strange anomaly that could be explained in any number of ways. Without the empty tomb, the appearances could have been dismissed as cases of wish fulfillment or hallucination or mistaken identity. Defenders of the resurrection of Jesus need both evidences.

## Swinburne's Argument

In his book *The Resurrection of God Incarnate* Oxford philosopher Richard Swinburne offers an interesting argument in support of the resurrection of Jesus.[3] He points out, as noted previously, that the two most crucial Christian theological claims are the incarnation and the resurrection of Jesus. He then argues (to the best of my knowledge this point has been made by no one else in Christian history) that each point supports the other. That is, Swinburne claims that the case for the resurrection of Jesus is strengthened if Jesus was God incarnate, and that the case that Jesus was God incarnate is strengthened if he was indeed raised from the dead.

Here is how the argument goes: if Jesus was indeed God incarnate, we would expect God to validate his person and ministry ("put his signature" on Jesus, as Swinburne puts it) by a "super-miracle" like raising him from the dead. And if Jesus was indeed raised by God from the dead, we would expect that Jesus would have had a unique and extraordinarily high status, like being the Son of God. (Notice that none of the great Old Testament heroes of faith—Abraham, Moses, King David, Isaiah, Jeremiah—was raised from the dead.) In other words, the claim that Jesus was raised is more likely if he was God incarnate, and the claim that he was God incarnate is more likely if he was raised.

## Two Additional Arguments

I conclude this chapter by suggesting two final arguments in favor of the resurrection of Jesus. They are related to but different from the points just made. First, in an argument briefly introduced in chapter three, we need to ask, What was the initial ignition that produced the Christian movement? Notice two obvious and patent facts: (1) there existed a phenomenon called first-century Judaism, and (2) a few years later there existed a phenomenon called the Christian church. Question: How do we get from one to the other?

As noted earlier, we live in a time when deflationary "lives of Jesus" are rampant (i.e., lives that deny or omit the incarnation and resurrection). Some scholars say that Jesus was essentially a teacher of wisdom, full of pithy aphorisms. Other say he was a healer and miracle worker. Others say that he was a prophet or preacher of Jewish apocalypticism. Others hold that he was an itinerant Cynic philosopher. One common thread is that such scholarly "lives of Jesus" do not affirm the resurrection.

And the problem is that it is hard to see why anybody would hold that such a relatively innocuous figure described in these "lives" was God incarnate. Surely Jesus scholars must posit a "life of Jesus" that would go at least some way toward explaining why the church so quickly arrived at startling ideas like Jesus' sinlessness, preexistence, divine Sonship and unity with God. Why did the movement that we now call the Christian church so quickly emerge? But if Jesus really was dead and later alive again, an answer to our question lies close at hand. That "super-miracle" (as Swinburne puts it) changed everything.

The second argument was also noted briefly; it has to do with certain accepted facts about New Testament events. So far as I can see, virtually every reputable scholar accepts the following points:

- that while first-century Jews were expecting a Messiah, the idea that the Messiah would die and be raised from the dead was unheard of prior to Jesus

- that Jesus died and was buried

- that Jesus' followers were discouraged, fearful and dejected

- that soon after the crucifixion of Jesus certain people were claiming that the tomb he had been buried in was empty

- that soon after the crucifixion of Jesus certain people were claiming to have seen Jesus

- that the followers of Jesus were transformed into bold and courageous preachers of the resurrection of Jesus and initiated a movement that grew to become the Christian church

The problem is that people who deny that Jesus was raised have a difficult time accounting for these facts. Indeed, this amounts to a major embarrassment for these folks: no one has ever succeeded in telling a story that both accounts for these known facts and makes sense. Indeed, most of the attempts to do so—Jesus did not die but only "swooned" and later recovered, the disciples unintentionally went to the wrong tomb, the disciples were hallucinating, somebody stole the body of Jesus—are all so weak as to collapse of their own weight once they are spelled out.[4]

The best way to account for these facts is to affirm that Jesus really was raised by God from the dead. In other words, there is a patch of first-century history that makes perfect sense from a Christian perspective but from no other.

## Conclusion

I agree with Swinburne. The resurrection was God's way of putting his stamp of approval of Jesus. It was a graphic way for God to underscore what the voice from heaven had said at Jesus' baptism: "This is my Son, the Beloved, with whom I am well pleased" (Matthew 3:17). Jesus is different from all others gurus, messiahs, prophets, spiritual teachers and religious founders of world history. He is the Son of God.

# 5

## DOES EVOLUTION DISPROVE CHRISTIANITY?

As everyone knows, the question of evolution and religion is controversial, to say the least. Opinions are held strongly and are located all over the map. I once spoke with a Christian student who was majoring in biology. She was troubled because the pastor of her family's Korean American home church firmly believed that if you took even one step toward evolution, you were, as he apparently put it, betraying Christ. She wondered whether you have to reject science if you are a Christian. But I also know science professors who seem to hold that to take even one step away from full-blown commitment to evolution is to sell out to fundamentalism and young earth creationism. Some even seem to think that if you are a legitimate scientist, you have to reject religion.

So what I plan to do in this chapter is simply to state and argue for my own views on the topic. They will not satisfy everyone. Moreover, I am conscious of the fact that I am not a scientist and that evolution is not my professional area.

## What Is Evolution?

Let's begin with the obvious fact that the word *evolution* can mean various things. Here are four: (1) In general usage, the term sometimes means something like progress, as for example when someone might say that the cell phone is evolving (i.e., improving) in some ways. (2) Moving to biology, sometimes the term means microevolution (i.e., descent with modification within species). We see this, for example, when bacteria change over time as a defense against antibiotics, or when certain physical traits of organisms change over time in response to environmental pressures (e.g., the famous cases of changes in the beaks of finches or the color of moth wings). (3) Sometimes the term refers to speciation and Charles Darwin's theory, which will be our central focus in this chapter, and which I will briefly explain in the next paragraph. (4) Finally, the term *evolution* sometimes refers to atheistic evolution or what is sometimes call "the grand evolutionary hypothesis." This is the idea that everything—and not just biological systems—evolved, including the universe and everything in it.

Darwin's theory first appeared in his 1859 book *The Origin of Species*.[1] The theory is based on the assumption of the common ancestry of all life, which itself is based on the anatomical and (as we now know) genetic similarities between all living things (e.g., the fact that all life has the same genetic code). The purpose of the theory is to explain the great diversity of life on earth. There are three main pillars of Darwin's theory as it is now generally understood (i.e., updated with some contemporary genetics). First, organisms undergo random genetic changes (where *random* means "unrelated to fitness"). These changes cause variations; they normally occur through mutations (i.e., changes in the DNA sequences of a cell genome that can be inherited), and sometimes by random genetic drift (i.e., genetic changes that have no influence on fitness but that nevertheless spread or disappear in a given population). Second, there is a process of natural selection of organisms and populations. That is, in competition for scarce resources, those organisms and species that are the fittest—that is, best adapted to their environments—will survive and reproduce. Third, there is self-replication. That is, genetic features are passed on to offspring. And because of natural selection, genetic features that provide competitive advantages survive. In other words, in a given population, those individuals that fit their environment best will, on average, thrive and produce the most offspring. The same applies to populations themselves. These three factors, Darwin argued—together of course with the natural laws and regularities in the universe—have produced, over long periods of time, complex and sophisticated organisms.

In relation to religion, the essential problem is this: the book of Genesis teaches that God created the heavens and the earth and the species that populate the earth, including human beings. But if Darwin is right, it is possible for apparently carefully designed organisms to be produced "blindly" (i.e., without an intelligent designer or any sort of technology). Darwin's great benefit to those who reject Genesis is that he provided a *theory* that allows as much. It is an entirely naturalistic theory; it does not require God or any intelligent designer. The importance of this result is well captured by Richard Dawkins, a contemporary scientist and defender of Darwin: "Although atheism might have been intellectually tenable before Darwin, Darwin made it possible to be an intellectually fulfilled atheist."[2]

My aim in this chapter is to argue that it is rationally possible to be a Christian who finds the religious truth in Scripture—a Christian, that is, of a fairly orthodox and traditional persuasion—and still affirm evolution.

## Evolution and Religion: The Options

What are the available options on this question? There appear to be five mains ones: young earth creationism, old earth creationism, intelligent design, theistic evolution (or evolutionary creationism) and atheistic evolution. I will speak briefly about each of them.

*Young earth creationism.* Young earth creationism is the theory held by fundamentalist Christians and others who read the Genesis creation accounts in a literalistic way; it is sometimes called "creation science." Its advocates hold that the universe and everything in it was created directly by God less than ten thousand years ago. Many accept the date given in the Scofield Bible (taken from seventeen-century Archbishop James Ussher's dating)[3] that the creation occurred in 4004 BC. They further hold that the "days" mentioned in Genesis 1 are literal twenty-four-hour days. They totally reject evolution, as well as the scientific evidence that the universe is some fourteen billion years old, that the earth is some four and a half billion years old, and that life first appeared on earth more than three billion years ago. They explain dinosaurs and other apparently ancient fossils (as well as geological strata) as artifacts of the worldwide flood described in Genesis 6–9, and that they also take literally. Young earth creationism has had several notable spokespersons, especially Henry Morris, Duane Gish and Ken Ham (and his group Answers in Genesis). They also have (at least) two museums that give their version of how things actually began.

One problem with this theory is that it is based on a literalistic biblical hermeneutic that few recognized biblical scholars countenance. Even certain authoritative ancient biblical exegetes (e.g., Origen and Augustine) rejected it. I myself take Genesis 1–3 seriously, but I take it primarily as a theology of creation rather than a science textbook. But to me the main criticism of young earth creationism is that it is far too dismissive of the findings of legitimate science to be taken seriously; that is, the evidence that young earth creationists are forced to reject is massive. Astronomers detect signals from stars and galaxies that are far, far older than ten thousand years ago; earth geology tells a coherent story that makes the earth far, far older than that; and some ancient tree rings, ice cores and even human pottery remains antedate 4004 BC. Moreover, this theory faces a big theological problem—namely, how to explain why a good and all-powerful God would allow the world to be filled with fake and radically misleading artifacts of an (apparent) ancient past.[4]

***Old earth creationism.*** Old earth creationists, like Hugh Ross and his group Reasons to Believe, are also usually conservative Christians, but they do not reject the scientific data in favor of the universe and the earth being billions of years old. But this theory, as the name implies, is a version of creationism. The universe exists because God created it, and human life exists because God directly created it. In other words, old earth creationists, like young earth creationists, reject common descent and evolution as explanations of the origin and development of life. They do not insist that the "days" mentioned in Genesis 1 are literal twenty-four-hour days, but they do accept Adam and Eve as actual historical figures. To some extent, old earth creationism overlaps with intelligent design at various points.

Beyond these crucial points, old earth creationism is a term that includes different points of view. Some who identify with it believe in the "gap theory" of creation. The idea is that there is a gap, not only linguistic but temporal, between the first verse in the Bible ("In the beginning when God created the heavens and the earth" [Genesis 1:1]) and the next verse ("the earth was a formless void"). Before the gap, billions of years ago, God created the universe, but then the earth was ruined (some say due to war between God and Satan); after the gap (and fairly recently) God intervened, repaired the earth and directly created life. Other old earth creationists believe in what we might call "progressive creation." The idea is that God does sometimes work through mechanisms like mutation and survival of the fittest, but frequently intervenes to influence the process and create new species. In other words, God performs different acts of creation of species at different points in geologic time. But while changes within species are accepted, the idea that evolution produces new species is rejected.

And that point would constitute my central reason for rejecting old earth creationism. The evidence in favor of evolution, and in favor of the claim that evolution over time produces new species, seems to me to be powerful.

*Intelligent design (ID).* Intelligent design has gained attention and even notoriety in recent years.[5] It is defended by scientists such as Michael Behe and Walter Bradley, philosophers like William Dembski and Stephen Meyer, and law professor Phillip Johnson. Its center of gravity is the Discovery Institute in Seattle. They accept science's findings on the age of the universe and of life, but they place great emphasis on evidence that they see of design or fine-tuning in the universe and especially in the cell. That is, the universe shows many signs of having been designed by an intelligent Creator for the purpose of producing life and intelligent life.[6] The cell is so complex that it cannot have been brought about by blind evolution alone. But many of the marks that ID people mention are found at the inorganic level (i.e., they are phenomena discussed by physicists and astronomers rather than biologists)—for example, the rate of expansion of the big bang, the value of the strong nuclear force, the value of the weak nuclear force, the strength of gravity, the expansion rate of the universe—and so could not have evolved biologically.[7] Although it is possible to believe both that there was intelligent design by

God and in evolution, it is important to note that defenders of ID are quite critical of Darwinian versions of biological evolution. They strongly doubt the idea that random mutations plus natural selection can produce complex organs and organisms, although some ID defenders accept variation and speciation once living things exist. All the ID defenders are theists, and most are Christians, but they insist that their arguments in favor of design are purely scientific. They do not identify the designer or designers that their arguments point to.

For example, biologist Michael Behe has introduced the idea of "irreducibly complex" systems and organs.[8] By that term he means such organs as the human eye (which puzzled Darwin himself) and bacterial flagella, as well as the organs and bodily systems that are responsible for blood clotting, bird flight and bat sonar. These are organs or systems with several interrelated parts, and whose workings are so complex and so dependent on the different parts being perfectly adjusted to each other that it is hard to imagine a successful evolutionary explanation of them. The different parts of the eye, for example, had to evolve separately, but one or two or even three parts of the eye would have no survival value at all for an organism without all the others arranged correctly and in working order. For example, there would be no evolutionary advantage if everything were there, in working order, except, say, the retina. Behe also argues that the recent revolution in cell biology (of which Darwin was ignorant) has shown great complexity and specificity in even the simplest of living cells. Another fruitful line of work has been pursued by mathematician and philosopher William Dembski.[9] He has done careful work on the question of how we go about recognizing design when we see it and what criteria have to be satisfied before we can legitimately consider something to be designed. He argues that the universe satisfies the necessary criteria and so was probably designed.

ID is often criticized by defenders of atheistic evolution (and by some theistic evolutionists) as fundamentalist creationism in disguise. (I think that criticism is unfair.) Critics also claim that the theory is not science at all, that its conclusions are not testable by the scientific method and thus it is not falsifiable. (This charge is of course disputed by ID people.)[10] It is also pointed out against ID that evidence against evolution (and in my opinion, some of ID's criticisms of evolution are plausible) is not necessarily evidence of design. Other critics of ID have argued that there are far too many imperfections in the overall design of life on earth for it to have been designed by a supremely intelligent and good designer. Why so much aggression, predation, violence and death in the natural world if it was designed by God? Why so many apparent mistakes in our genome if we were designed by God (e.g., our bodies' inability, unlike other primates, to manufacture vitamin C to prevent scurvy?)[11]

I have a great deal of respect for ID, but in the end I do not identify with it. One important reason has to do with irreducible complexity. Of course there are complex organs like the eye or wing that will not function if one component is removed. And certainly all the components had to evolve. It is true that absent a designer the separate parts could not have evolved with their future functions in the eye or wing being (so to speak) aimed at. But nothing rules out the possibility that the individual parts were adaptive and thus evolved for other reasons. In other words, they might have been functional for the organism in other contexts.[12] Indeed, Michael Ruse gives an example: the Krebs cycle. This is a complicated but well-understood biochemical process by which energy from food is converted into a form that is usable to cells. This cycle, Ruse says, "was cobbled together out of other cellular processes that do other things. It was a 'bricolage.' Each one of the bits and pieces of the cycle exists for other purposes and has been co-opted for the new end." In other words, many complex systems have been "put in place by selection."[13]

And although this next point does not refute ID, I have always wondered when or how the intelligent designer is supposed to intervene. One possibility is that the designer set it all up ahead of time, much like Leibniz's pre-established harmony. In other words, the evolution of life was predestined in all its details by the designer. But of course this means that empirically the development of life will probably look no different than it would look if it were not designed at all (i.e., as if the atheistic evolutionists are correct). So it looks as if ID must posit a series of interventions—to produce new species, perhaps—from time to time. And that makes me wonder when and how often and precisely how the designer intervenes. Defenders of ID, so far as I know, do not try to answer this question, and that is understandable. Still, to me it is a genuine puzzle, if ID is true.

***Theistic evolution (also sometimes called evolutionary creationism).*** Theistic evolution amounts to the theory that God exists and created the universe (some fourteen billion years ago). Since then, the universe has developed via natural means, for example, through astronomical change (the big bang, then gasses, then galaxies, then stars, then planets). The earth developed via geological and chemical change. And life developed via the mechanisms of Darwinian evolution. In other words, God designed the universe so that life would naturally evolve; evolution was the main method used by God. Purpose was involved. God may or may not have intervened occasionally (e.g., to alter or speed up the process), but unlike in intelligent design, divine interventions in the processes play no big role in the theory. Natural causes are taken to be adequate explanations. In fact, some prefer to emphasize God's immanence (i.e., God's constant watch over and providential involvement in all earthly affairs) as opposed to occasional interventions. In particular, human beings descended from prehuman ancestors, and in some mysterious way were implanted with the image of God. Francis Collins is a noted defender of theistic evolution, along with the organization BioLogos. And, as noted, I identify myself with this theory.

**Atheistic evolution (or the grand evolutionary hypothesis).** Atheistic evolution is the theory advocated by such luminaries as Stephen J. Gould, Richard Dawkins and Daniel Dennett. It is not just a scientific theory but a worldview or philosophy of life; that is, it gives confident answers to all questions, even questions about morality and the meaning of life. God does not exist, and everything that has ever happened occurred through in-principle scientifically explicable ways. The theory is based on metaphysical naturalism.[14] The universe in some form has always existed or else it came into existence spontaneously (e.g., from gravity itself or from a subatomic vacuum seething with quantum particles); life emerged chemically; and life and human life evolved by Darwinian methods exclusively. Life and advanced life evolved "blindly" (i.e., with no plan or purpose). Nature took life from molecules to humans with no help from God.

Defenders of atheistic evolution often imply that if you believe in evolution you have to believe in the grand evolutionary hypothesis. But that is not true. Old Testament scholar David Atkinson says,

> Clearly, if "evolution" is lifted out of the sphere of biological hypothesis where it is open to scientific investigation, and is elevated to the status of a whole world-view of the way things are, then there is direct conflict with biblical faith. But if "evolution" remains at the level of scientific biological

hypothesis, it would seem that there is little reason for conflict between the implications of Christian belief in the Creator and the scientific explorations of the way which—at the level of biology—God has gone about his creating processes.[15]

## What Makes a Scientific Theory Acceptable?

How do we go about deciding whether a certain scientific theory, or any theory, is acceptable?[16] This is a complicated question, much discussed in the philosophy of science. I will focus on five important criteria. The first and most important criterion is *fit with the evidence*. If a theory is inconsistent with or made improbable by the evidence that is available to us (which includes evidence that is directly relevant to the theory and all other known facts), then the theory is to be rejected. A second criterion is that an acceptable theory must be *falsifiable*. Of course if a theory is true, it will not be falsified. But the point is that there must be a potential way that it could be shown to be false if it is false. A third criterion is *predictive power*. As scientists often observe, a good theory is one that allows us to make accurate predictions about what will happen in the future under specified conditions. A fourth criterion is *explanatory power*. This is closely related to predictive power but, as we will see shortly, is not quite the same thing. A good theory explains as many of the facts that we see before us as possible. If a theory has too many anomalies ("nomological danglers"), it is not a good theory. A fifth criterion is *simplicity*. There is a principle in philosophy called the principle of parsimony (PP). The idea is that if you've got two competing theories that are apparently equal according to the other criteria, you should accept the simpler theory. PP is a recommendation rather than a proof, but it has proved to be fruitful in the history of science. But PP immediately raises the question of what simplicity for a theory amounts to. That is not easy to say, and I am not going to explore the issue further here.

How does evolution stack up in relation to these five criteria? Despite the fact that I am a defender of evolution—as noted, I identify myself as a theistic evolutionist—the answer is that its scoring overall is solid but not as strong as its defenders would like. As far as fit with the fossil evidence is concerned, it seems to me that the fossil record supports evolution, but not overwhelmingly so. For many species, evolutionists sometimes tell "just so" stories that are not strongly supported by the fossil record. In addition, many species seem to have appeared suddenly at various points in the past, with no previous intermediate steps.[17] These are large claims, to be sure, and defenders of evolution will dispute them. They will quite rightly point out that the fossil record is necessarily spotty and incomplete, and that in many cases intermediate stages between species are there.[18] That is, there are many cases (e.g., the whale) where the fossils tell the evolutionary story amazingly well.[19]

What about fit with the genetic evidence? Here, I think, the new Darwinian view that combines genetics with evolution fares much better. The fact that virtually all life shares genetic coding, and shares the same biochemistry of DNA and proteins, is a powerful argument for common descent.[20] And scientists now hold that all sequences of DNA, and the information they contain, can be produced by natural processes. As Freeland suggests, "the standard genetic code at work in modern cells may be a product of substantial evolution that had taken place by about 3 billion years ago."[21] And Alexander claims that even "if there were no fossils at all, we would still be able to construct much of evolutionary history just from genetics."[22]

What about falsifiability? Here evolution clearly passes. We can imagine many events that, if they occurred, would disprove the theory. For example, suppose paleontologists discovered human bones left over from the Jurassic Period (with no catastrophic earth events to indicate mixing up of strata). Evolution would be in big trouble.

On the third criterion, predictive power, it seems to me that evolution does only fairly well. Because of the huge time periods that Darwinian evolution requires, as well as our ignorance of what evolutionary pressures a population might face in the future, the theory does not allow us to make much in the way of accurate predictions about its future. It is occasionally possible to make fairly vague predictions about where evolution is going to take a particular species—that is, that a given organism will develop resistance to drugs or will find a certain ecological niche—but that is about all.

But on the fourth criterion, explanatory power, evolution excels. Indeed, the great strength of the theory is that it is enormously successful in explaining the history of life and the great variations of life forms. So much is this true that all of the life sciences as they exist today simply presuppose evolution. The theory explains, in a powerful way, how and why species got to the point where they are now. If we were to reject evolution, as several of the theories just discussed recommend, we would have to rewrite all of the life sciences. In my opinion that would be an enormously high cost to pay. Evolution as a theory is very well entrenched. It greatly helps scientists not only to explain biological change and variation, but also to classify organisms, to explain similarities and differences between organisms, and to explain odd biological observations. This to me is the strongest argument in favor of evolution.

Even if we were clear on what simplicity for a theory in a specific science consists of, it seems to me that the fifth criterion has limited relevance to the current debate. If young earth creationism were pretty much equal to the other theories according to the first three criteria—which it is not—it could surely be ruled out on the grounds of simplicity. But between old earth creationism, intelligent design, theistic evolution and atheistic evolution, it seems to me that considerations of simplicity will not help a great deal.

## Problems with Evolutionary Theory

Despite the fact that I endorse evolution (but not of course atheistic evolution), I want to be honest about what I take to be the weaknesses in the theory. Microevolution is no problem; so far as I know, everybody accepts it, even young earth creationists. Common descent: I think the evidence is convincing. Descent with modification: again, no problem. What then are the main problems with evolution? I would say there are three: (1) What was the origin of life? (2) Can evolution produce new species? and (3) How can we explain the often quite sudden appearance in the fossil record of new and fully formed populations of animal life?

On the first question—the origin of life—obviously Darwinian evolution by itself cannot answer it. Mutation plus natural selection cannot generate life from nonlife since the theory only applies to already living things. However, those who are committed to the grand evolutionary hypothesis (as well as others) insist that under certain circumstances life can be naturally produced and that this is what happened on earth some three billion years ago. Indeed, there is much speculation in chemistry about how this might be possible. Many scientists and nonscientists are interested in this question; there even exists a scientific group called the International Society for Study of Origin of Life.

Probably the most popular current theory is that light/electrical storms billions of years ago generated molecules like the DNA-RNA bases (the famous Miller-Urey experiment from the 1950s). But this suggestion has been strongly criticized.[23] Another idea that Graham Cairns-Smith promoted is that an inorganic template (perhaps clay) catalyzed a molecule assembly of organic compounds, which later were able to replicate themselves. Some imagine an "RNA world" before DNA, since RNA has some of the properties of DNA and proteins, but the trouble here is that RNA is much less stable than DNA. So there are several ideas, but none of them look compelling.

I personally believe that God created life, and, as noted, none of the proposals made thus far have gained much approval in the scientific community. That is, there seems to exist no satisfactory theory that explains the development of organic chemistry out of inorganic. But I am more than willing to allow scientists to continue to search for a natural explanation. And I do not consider the fact that Darwinian evolution cannot tell us how life emerged as a deficiency in the theory. It certainly is a deficiency in the grand evolutionary hypothesis, however.[24] Moreover, I do not see any crisis for theology if life did emerge naturally.

The second question—whether mutation plus natural selection can produce new species—amounts to a criticism that defenders of ID raise.[25] And it is certainly true that microevolution—which everybody admits—does not by itself amount to species change. But it is obvious that new species do appear in the fossil record and that the record contains fewer transitional forms than defenders of evolution would like there to be. Still, I have no problem giving evolution a pass on this point. I accept that speciation can be a natural process.

The third question—which has to do with the fossil record— seems to many people, both critics and defenders of evolution, to be the Achilles' heel of Darwin's own notion of gradual change. What the fossil record seems to show is that species can appear suddenly, do not change much during their time in existence and then go extinct. That is, many species (like the Burgess Shale fauna) appear suddenly and fully formed (i.e., with no previous gradual evolution that we can see evidence of). This problem is recognized by both critics and defenders of evolution. One important reaction to the fact was the development of a theory called "punctuated equilibrium" (punk eek) in the 1970s. The most famous figure in this movement was Stephen Jay Gould. Punctuated equilibrium gives up on Darwinian gradualism, but is still a version of biological evolution based on Darwin's three central tenets (see the first section of this chapter). The main point that Gould and his allies were making is that most fossil species remain unchanged for relatively long periods (this is called "statis"), and that when change occurs it is relatively rapid (by geological time scales).[26] Everybody, even Darwin, has always known that species can disappear rapidly, but now it is affirmed that evolution allows for rapid speciation. There have been many debates about the mechanisms of rapid evolutionary change, and I think it is safe to say that no consensus has yet been reached. In the end, I believe that punctuated equilibrium does more to underscore the difficulty than solve it.

Anybody who is interested in the topic I am discussing will have noticed that defenders of evolution are extraordinarily determined and vociferous in defending the theory against critics. (Perhaps this is in part explained as a reaction to ID's "wedge strategy" of attempting to influence school science curricula.) Many insist that evolution is not a theory at all but a scientifically established fact. But when asked to substantiate that claim, they usually point to instances of microevolution, which of course everybody accepts anyway. Or perhaps they just have common descent in mind. But if I can put it this way, microevolution does not prove evolution. It bothers me, as a believer in evolution, that many of its defenders seem quite unwilling to admit that there are any nontrivial problems with the theory. I am not the first to make this point, but it almost seems as if evolution now counts as secular academia's creation myth. I confess to agreeing with Phillip Johnson's claim that part of the apparent dogmatism of evolution's defenders is the thought that apart from evolution there is no scientific alternative to intelligent design and God. And atheistic evolutionists definitely do not want to allow that possibility. Accordingly, if you are an atheist, evolution is the only game in town. Despite its flaws, there is no better theory available.

## Being a Christian and Accepting Evolution

Let's return to the biology major I spoke with years ago; she was concerned about being both a Christian and a scientist. One of the issues that her young earth creationist pastor brought up, and which also concerned her, was the idea that if you bought into evolution, you would have to toss out Genesis 1–3. And if you did that, you would also have to toss out any robust notion of biblical authority. And if you did that, there would be no reason to be a Christian. Accordingly, I do need to say something about that issue.

The vast majority of Christians who reject evolution do so on biblical grounds. They take Genesis 1:1–2:3 to be a scientifically accurate description of how God created. It is a kind of science textbook. But along with very many biblical scholars, I do not interpret the text in that way. Note that we are not talking here about biblical authority; I too hold the Bible to be the Word of God and to be, when properly interpreted, infallible on all matters of Christian faith and practice. We are talking instead about biblical hermeneutics (i.e., biblical interpretation). Notice further that the Bible as a whole contains texts that fit into a great variety of genres—among others, there are law codes, histories, prophecies, wise sayings, poems, oracles, Gospels, parables, sermons, letters and apocalyptic books. Although many parts of the Bible clearly do want to be read as literally true, as I read Genesis 1 it does not seem to me to read as if it were meant to be literally true science. Indeed, it reads more like a kind of hymn or poem. Note the repeated formulas, like the refrains "God said," "and God saw that it was good," "let there be," and "it was so." Also, there are anomalies in the text from a scientific point of view. Of course, an omnipotent God could make sure that there was light (Genesis 1:1) before there were any natural sources of light like the sun and the moon (Genesis 1:14-19). Of course an omnipotent God could make sure that there were plants (Genesis 1:11-12) before there was any rain, which it would seem was possible only when the sun and the earth's atmosphere existed (Genesis 1:16). But these points still seem odd. And the second is made even odder by Genesis 2:5, where it says that there were no plants until God caused it to rain.

In the end I agree with John Collins. He says that Genesis 1 is

> what we may call *exalted prose narrative*. This name for the genre will serve us in several ways. First, it acknowledges that we are dealing with prose narrative . . . which will include the making of truth claims about the world in which we live. Second, by calling it exalted, we are recognizing that . . . we must not impose a "literalistic" hermeneutic on the text.[27]

What this means is that Genesis 1 does not require us to hold that God created the universe in six twenty-four-hour days, nor does it rule out the possibility that the universe is billions of years old.

Collins notes that Genesis 1 makes truth claims. Indeed it does. This is where I should explain my claim above that Genesis 1–3 is primarily not a science of creation but a theology of creation. So what are those truth claims? I will mention five: (1) The universe exists because God brought it into existence;

accordingly, naturalism, pantheism, panentheism, emanationism and the idea that the universe has always existed are all false theories of creation. (2) God's creation was originally very good; accordingly, cosmic dualistic theories like Zoroastrianism are false. (3) Human beings are special in the creation because only they were created "in the image of God" (Genesis 1:27). (4) Human beings disobey God, and God judges sin, but (5) God also has mercy on sinners.

All right, then, what about Adam and Eve? Were they actual historical people who lived long ago (maybe in the Pleistocene or the Neolithic Periods)? The issue is made more complex by the fact that Paul (Romans 5:12-21; 1 Corinthians 15:21-22, 47, 49; Acts 17:26) speaks about Adam as if he were a real historical person. Apart from those New Testament references, I myself would be much inclined to believe that the Adam and Eve in Genesis were meant to be metaphors or symbols of the entire human race; their fall into sin is a way of underscoring the truth that "all have sinned and fall short of the glory of God" (Romans 3:23). But perhaps Adam and Eve really existed. I do not see why they could not be both historical figures and archetypes. Now surely the fossil and genetic evidence powerfully supports the idea that humans evolved from more primitive apelike creatures in the Pleistocene Epoch. Perhaps Adam and Eve were the first members of the species Homo sapiens who were transformed spiritually by an encounter with God, by being endowed with the image of God and by being receiving moral commands from God.

## Conclusion

So the answers to the questions we began with are (1) no, evolution does not disprove Christianity; (2) yes, you can rationally believe in evolution and be a Christian; and (3) yes, you can be both a scientist and a Christian. In my opinion, evolution represents one significant way God has chosen to bring about complex life, including human beings.[28]

# CAN COGNITIVE SCIENCE EXPLAIN RELIGION?

It is not often that new topics and debates emerge in the philosophy of religion. But one such subject of study arises from the cognitive science of religion (CSR), which is a loosely organized group of cognitive psychologists, neuroscientists, evolutionary biologists and others who are interested in the phenomenon of religion.[1] They have been arguing that religion is natural. That is, human beings have a natural tendency to believe in the existence of God, gods or other supernatural spirits who are taken to provide moral guidance and to issue rewards and punishments to human beings.[2] These scholars argue that such beliefs are adaptive, for individuals and groups, in an evolutionary sense. Accordingly, the fact that religion is extraordinarily widespread among human groups is exactly what should be expected. My project, in this chapter, is to determine as best I can whether religious belief is indeed natural.

## Religion as Natural

Let's take it that the CSR scholars are arguing that

(1) Human beings have a natural tendency to believe in
    the existence of God, gods or other supernatural
    beings.

I want to begin the chapter with this question: If proposition
(1) is true, is this good news or bad news for religion? It seems that
the argument might go either way. For example, we might take (1)
to be a friendly amendment to the views of religion that religious
people have because it seems to rule out the idea (often suggested
by opponents of religion) that religious belief is unnatural because
it is irrational. It might also be taken to render unrealistic the
vision of many atheists of a totally secular human society. If (1) is
true, it seems that religion is here to stay.

But the argument can be pushed in the other direction too.
Religious people might take (1) to be an attempt, not unlike the
venerable "projection" theories of Feuerbach, Marx and Freud, to
"explain" the phenomenon of religion by explaining it away. That
is, if (1) is true, it can be argued that religion is widespread not
because supernatural agents really do exist but because cognitive
or evolutionary mechanisms cause or at least strongly incline
human beings to believe in them. In reading the writings of CSR
scholars, one does gain the impression that the explanation of the
phenomenon of religion that they offer is, in their view, the only
one that is available or necessary.[3]

Years ago, I had a student who I will call Peter. He was a senior,
a bright and incisive psychology and philosophy major. Raised in
a religious family, the son of a Christian minister, he himself was
unable to believe. His doubts were too strong. But the odd fact
was that he *wanted* to believe. His religious skepticism deeply
troubled him; part of him envied the faith of his parents. As we
spoke, I discovered that what most troubled him was the fact that
religious experiences can apparently be explained naturalistically.
I tried to tell him that the mere fact that it is possible to provide

plausible-sounding atheistic explanations of religious experiences (e.g., somebody's sense of being close to God or forgiven by God or rescued by God) does not entail that those explanations are true. Perhaps complete explanations *would* involve God.

A further point: CSR explanations of religion challenge the rationality of religious beliefs—so it is said—because the mechanisms that produce beliefs in supernatural agents are not reliable sources of true beliefs. This is because (again, so it is said) people have the tendency described in (1) for nontruth-related reasons; they believe in the supernatural either because humans are cognitively hardwired to do so or because it is advantageous in an evolutionary sense for them to do so (or belief is a spandrel of what evolution has selected).[4] (We will explore some such arguments shortly.) Accordingly, on this interpretation of (1), it can be concluded that human beings created God (and other supernatural agents), not vice versa.

But before exploring further the question of whether (1), if true, is good news or bad news, we must first ask whether (1) is true. And that of course will obviously depend to a great extent on what the word *natural* means. Equally obviously, there has been much discussion in recent philosophy over the meaning of such terms as *natural* and *naturalism*. I will enter that debate only to the extent of offering a distinction among three different senses of the word *natural*, a distinction that I hope will be sufficiently helpful to support what I want to say in this paper.

**Natural *as explainable*.** To say that something—an event, let's say (which would include the event of someone's coming to have a belief)—is natural might mean that it is part of the natural order (i.e., that it can be studied by science, is replicable and can at least in principle be explained by methods similar to those used in the natural sciences). It is not random or miraculous or totally inexplicable. For example, many proponents of CSR are much inclined to say that religious belief is natural because it can be explained in evolutionary terms (i.e., it promotes survival).

**Natural** *as easy.* To say that something is natural—in this case I am thinking more of beliefs or opinions than events—might be to say that it is easy to learn and transmit to others. The belief amounts to common sense; we have it without constraint or even without giving much thought to it. The belief—so we might say— "comes naturally"; we do not have to reason our way toward it (although perhaps we could do so if necessary). To say that a belief is natural in this second sense is not to say that it must be true; presumably it was once natural in this sense to believe that the earth is flat.

**Natural** *as appropriate.* Notice that so far we have no necessary connection to truth and falsity; a belief could be natural in the first or second sense and be either true or false; a belief could be unnatural in the first or second sense and be either true or false. But let me suggest a third possible definition of *natural* (one that admittedly has little "ordinary language" warrant) that *does* have such a connection. To say that a belief is natural might also be to affirm that it is appropriate; it is a correct appreciation of what is in fact the case. On this third notion a natural belief is one that is either clearly true or at least rational given what the person having the belief knows or ought to know. It is epistemologically justifiable. Thus we might say that it is natural to believe that the external world is real or that other human beings have minds.[5]

So now we can turn to our main question: Is religious belief natural? That is, in which, if any, of these three senses is religious belief natural? I will first distinguish between two sorts of religious belief. I will call "generic religious belief" (GRB) the simple belief in supernatural beings or spirits of some sort. So GRB amounts to acceptance of (1). I will call "full-blown religious belief" (FBRB) the acceptance of the beliefs and practices of actual religions (e.g.,

Christianity, Judaism, Islam, Buddhism, etc).[6] (Theistic religions and most other full-blown religions accept versions of GRB, but not all do [e.g., some versions of Buddhism].) I make this distinction because in my view the answer to our original question—Is religious belief natural?—will turn out to be different depending on which sort of religious belief we are talking about.

Believers and nonbelievers will surely disagree about the question. What might nonbelievers say? On the first definition of *natural*, I suspect that most nonreligious people would be inclined to say yes, both as to GRB and FBRB. Much ink has been spilled by such folk in the hope of explaining the phenomenon of religious belief. Religious belief is natural—so they will say—because its presence can be explained by psychological or sociological or cognitive or evolutionary mechanisms.[7] The point they are implicitly making is that religious belief is *not* to be explained by the presence of sufficient evidence or convincing arguments in its favor. And I think nonreligious people will also be inclined to affirm that religion of both sorts is natural in the second sense. They will admit that it is easy for most human beings to be religious, especially if one is born into a religious family or community. But nonbelievers will almost certainly deny that GRB and FBRB are natural in the third sense. They will instead hold that religious belief systematically misreads the way reality is. Gods—so they will say—are products of human imagination.[8]

What might religious believers say? I think that would very much depend on what sort of religion we are talking about. Virtually all religious people, one suspects, would insist that religious belief is natural in the sense of being appropriate, or at least that their own full-blown religious beliefs are. I will return to this point later. But I think Christian believers ought to have a more nuanced answer to questions about whether Christian religious belief is either explainable or easy. I, at least, am unable to answer that question unequivocally; I want to argue that GRB is largely explainable and for many people easy, but that Christian belief (as well as beliefs in many other actual religions) is neither.[9]

## Why Are People Religious?

It is clear that religious beliefs and practices are extraordinarily widespread among human beings. They are found in all cultures and nations and periods of history. Religion seems easy to acquire and to transmit to others; *Homo sapiens* is sometimes called *Homo religious*. This is not to say that religion is universal; there are irreligious people and largely secular communities in the world (e.g., communities of intellectual and cultural elites in contemporary Europe and North America).

But why are the vast majority of people religious? Why do people need and practice religion? Lots of possibilities have been suggested. Is it in order to understand the universe and our place in it? Or is it to try to escape misfortune in life? Or is it to assuage our sense of guilt? Or is it to provide some sort of meaning in life? Or is it to assure us of survival of death? Or is it more than one or all of these? Whatever the reason or reasons, it seems that religious belief among human beings, while certainly avoidable, is largely both easy and explainable. In those senses it does seem to me natural to believe in some sort of God, gods or supernatural forces. (I will return to why I think certain actual religions, especially Christianity, are not natural in these senses.)

There is a strange phenomenon in the neighborhood.[10] With the third sense of *natural* in mind, it seems that on most topics (excluding, perhaps, religion and politics) sensible people who disagree can usually understand and appreciate the position of the other person, maybe even the evidence or arguments of the other person, even though they may disagree strongly. But here the situation is different. Nonbelievers often hold that beliefs like "God exists" or "God created the universe" are irrational. They have a hard time understanding how any sensible person could believe such claims. But the reverse is true too: many religious believers (theists, anyway) will insist that such claims are clearly true; their experience (or purported experience) of God is such that they have a hard time understanding how any sensible person could deny these claims.

It is even the case that religious believers and nonbelievers occasionally offer interesting explanations of the behavior of people in the other group. Religious folk can suggest that nonbelievers are blinded by pride, self-interest and their own sinfulness; they do not *want* God to exist, so they deny that God exists. And skeptics can argue that religious people are rendered naive and credulous by their powerful need to believe in a loving and avuncular heavenly Father who cares for them and will reward them with eternal life. That is why they believe.

Both these arguments, if taken to be refutations of the positions being commented on, are fallacious. You cannot refute a belief B by arguing—even correctly arguing—that B is caused by x.

Nevertheless, let's think about this last point for a bit. Religious believers do sometimes express puzzlement at religious unbelief. Christians among them might accordingly ask this question: Why do certain people who hear and understand the Christian message reject it? This is a puzzle to them for three reasons: (1) they think the Christian message is true; (2) they think that it is in the interest of all people to accept it; and (3) the Bible at least seems to suggest that in some sense all people know certain aspects of the Christian message.

Where does Scripture say this? In the early chapters of the book of Romans Paul is trying to show that all people—both Jews and Gentiles—are guilty before God and are "without excuse"

(Romans 1:20). In this context, he writes, "What can be known about God is plain to them [i.e., to those who, as Paul says, 'by their wickedness suppress the truth'], because God has shown it to them" (Romans 1:19). But what exactly did Paul mean by this? The claim seems nonintuitive. How has God "shown it to them"?

Let's begin an attempt to answer these questions by asking what Christians think "can be known about God" naturally (i.e., apart from revelation). Obviously, that can be disputed. But in order to keep things simple, we'll call it proposition (2):

(2) God exists and is the all-powerful and all-knowing Creator of the heavens and the earth, and God is worthy of worship and obedience.

But in what sense is (2), or something like it, "plain" to all people? There certainly seem to be sincere atheists, agnostics and members of nontheistic religions who do not know proposition (2) at all. They don't even *believe* it. It would be odd and perhaps even insulting if I were to say to one of my atheist colleagues at the Claremont Colleges, "The existence of God is plain to you; indeed, you *know* that (2) is true." So we again wonder what Paul might have meant.

One clue is that Paul seems to have thought that religious unbelief is a spiritual rather than intellectual problem. Thus he goes on to write:

Ever since the creation of the world his eternal and divine nature, invisible though they are, have been understood and seen through the things he has made. So they are without excuse; for though they knew God, they did not honor him as God or give thanks to him, but they became futile in their thinking, and their senseless minds were darkened. (Romans 1:20-21)

Let us say that an *intellectual problem* is one that is solvable by the right application of human reason, learning and experience. And let us say that a *spiritual problem* is one that is solved by being rightly related to God. Paul seems to have thought that religious unbelief is a matter of being wrongly related to God. To borrow Pascal's famous distinction, it is more a matter of the heart than of the mind.

Note Paul's phrase "their senseless minds were darkened." The Bible has a common metaphor for this phenomenon; it is called "hardening of the heart." The *heart* is the Bible's term for the innermost location of human knowledge, emotions, decisions, and sense of right and wrong. Hardness of heart is a kind of stubbornness or indifference toward a claim or toward a recommended action; it is a refusal to admit it or a culpable failure to understand it, perhaps by a willful misconstrual of it. In the Bible it is essentially human resistance to see the hand of God at work or to accept the will of God (Matthew 13:13-15). Where a person refuses *no matter what* to believe a certain claim made by God or live in ways required by God, that is hardness of heart.[11]

## Different Senses of *Know*

We are trying to understand Paul's claim that "what can be known about God is plain to them." The problem is that it is not easy to see how this claim can be true. Let us see whether we can make any progress on this point.

In philosophy there are different senses of the word *know*. Let me propose a distinction; let us call all those uses of the expression "A knows p" that entail "A believes p" *strong senses* of *know*. But there are also *weak senses* of the word—that is, senses in which knowing p does not entail believing p, or at least not consciously believing p. Perhaps there are different ways of understanding this weak sense. It may be a matter of rejecting p consciously and believing it unconsciously. Perhaps it is a matter of wavering back and forth—believing it some of the time and rejecting it at other times. It might be akin to those cases of people who in all sincerity deny that they are racists yet show racist attitudes in psychological tests.[12] It might even be a case of believing it with one part of the brain and rejecting it with another.

An illustration: if I may speak personally, I am quite sure that before I became a Christian years ago, I knew (in the weak sense) certain things about myself that I was then quite unwilling to believe. These were things that I was afraid might be true about my own propensity for pride, self-centeredness, lust and violence. Sometimes in life we see what we want to see. You might say that I knew these things but did not believe them. Only after identifying myself as a Christian did I come to know, in the strong sense, these truths about myself.

Accordingly, I think it is quite possible for the following three claims to be true for some person A and claim p:

(3) A knows p (in the weak sense).

(4) A does not know p (in the strong sense).

And

(5) A *ought* to know p (in the strong sense); that is, A is culpable for not knowing p (in the strong sense).

In high school I knew a student who was, frankly, well on his way to becoming a violent and malicious person. But his mother, who I also knew, was unwilling to face the truth about him. I suspect that she knew, in the weak sense, the truth about her son, but not in the strong sense. She was always making excuses for him, overlooking his misdeeds, claiming that his behavior was just a passing phase he would outgrow. Her unwillingness consciously to face the truth was, I think, at least somewhat culpable. In the weak sense, I think she knew that he was a bad person; but she did not consciously believe it, and she *should* have believed it.

So the situation is as follows: According to Christians the truth is that

(2) God exists and is the all-powerful and all-knowing Creator of the heavens and the earth, and God is worthy of worship and obedience.

(6) Everybody knows (in the weak sense) that (2) is true.

And

(7) Those who do not know (2) in the strong sense are culpable for their ignorance.

Proposition (2) is a truth that unbelievers do not want to admit, so they refuse to accept it. They harden their hearts against it. The problem is essentially spiritual rather than intellectual. It exists not in the state of the evidence but rather in human beings. We have a defect that prevents us from seeing the truth, from knowing (2) in the strong sense.

That defect is called *pride*. There is of course a positive sense of the word pride: "You should take pride in your work." But I refer here to the negative sense, as in sayings like "Pride goes before a fall." In this context pride includes desiring to control one's own life and firmly setting one's will against someone else being in charge, even if that person has the right to be in charge.

What I am proposing here is one possible interpretation of Paul's words. On this interpretation the idea is that spiritual considerations prevent people from knowing in the strong sense certain truths that would otherwise be clear to them. Visual metaphors naturally come into play here. Of the existence and glory of God the nonbeliever says, "I just don't see it." The believer says, "Your eyes need to be opened." Nonbelievers who convert and become believers frequently say things like "It was as if blinders were removed from my eyes; I can now see what I did not see."

## Religion as Costly

I am claiming that Christian belief (as well as belief in other religions) is not natural in the first and second senses of *natural*. Why do I do so? Because if critics of religion were correct that we created God rather than vice versa, it seems to me that the Christian God is not the sort of divinity we would create. More broadly, if religion is an entirely human product (a product, say, of evolution plus culture), the Christian religion (as well as others) is not the sort of religion that we would create. Well then, on my view, what sort of supernatural beings would human beings naturally create?

There are lots of possibilities. One would be a legalistic God or gods—that is, a God who promulgates a set of laws governing human behavior. Obey those laws—so this religion would say— and God will bless you; disobey them and you are in trouble. Another possibility is a God or gods who must be appeased by ritual. Our primary responsibility is to perform the correct ceremonials correctly—so such a religion would say—do that and the gods will be appeased and will bless you; fail to do so and you will be cursed. A third possibility, much in the spirit of our age, would be a God who is, so to speak, maximally accepting and ecumenical. Whatever your religious beliefs and practices, as long as you follow them sincerely, you will be all right.

I accept the idea that GRB may well be largely natural in our first and second senses of *natural*. But I hold that Christian belief (as well as, surely, certain other sorts of FBRB) is not. It is, so to speak, too costly. Some of the costs are evolutionary and some are not. In other words, when we get to Christianity (and other forms of FBRB), as opposed to bare GRB, some of the beliefs are counterintuitive and many of the practices are maladaptive.

What are the evolutionary disadvantages? Well, think of the time, effort and material expenses that a religious person must typically invest; there are often rules about food, dress, work, charitable giving and attendance at ceremonies; sometimes it can even be painful or highly self-denying to be religious (think of celibate priests and nuns, as well as martyrs). Not only are there costs involved here, there are also no apparent or obvious evolutionary advantages that religion bestows on its adherents.

But the costliness of religion is a point that cognitive and evolutionary critics of religion are well aware of. In their effort to provide a plausible naturalistic explanation of the phenomenon of religion, they have mounted a counterattack. When looked at carefully (so they say), religion *is* adaptive; it *does* bestow evolutionary advantages. The increased cooperation and cohesion that we see in religious groups is obviously beneficial to their members. The same is true of the altruistic behavior that most religions encourage. Such other benefits are listed as mating opportunities, improved health, survivorship, economic opportunities, psychological well-being and assistance during crises.[13] Moreover, the very costliness of religion may itself bestow an evolutionary advantage to persons because these costs tend to limit the number of "freeloaders" who pretend to be religious in order to reap the advantages but are not sincere. Accordingly, costliness is a plus for religion.[14]

It is doubtless true that there are benefits to being religious and that the costliness of religion can itself have evolutionary benefits. But are they enough to outweigh the costs? I do not think so. At a minimum I want to claim that it is not clear that they do. (Of course each of the points that I mention about the relative weight of the costs and benefits would have to be tested empirically, if possible, which I admittedly make no attempt to do on this occasion.)[15]

In addition to the points noted earlier, it is clear that those who accept Christian claims about God and know them in the strong sense must do several things that human beings do not normally want to do. I do not claim that all these next points are evolutionary or fitness costs, but they do amount to challenges to human pride and sense of autonomy. What are those things? I will mention five of them. First, such folk must believe in certain things that they cannot see or touch or prove. Second, they must humble themselves and admit that they owe their lives to the One who created them. Third, they must submit to the moral authority of their Creator and repent of their wrongdoing. Fourth, they must both worship and obey the commands of the One who created them. Fifth, they must place their trust in God rather than in themselves. Pride works to prevent all five.[16]

Why then are Christians (as well as members of other religions) willing to endure the required costs? Surely the crucial point that decides whether a person will be religious in a FBRB sense is not the set of benefits that might accrue from having the relevant beliefs—it is the question whether the person holds that the statement "God exists," as well as other required beliefs, is true. Belief in God, like my belief that grass is green and that my granddaughter loves me, is not undertaken for any purpose or benefit at all.[17] Only if a person genuinely believes in God is he or she likely willingly to incur the costs of being a theist. So even if the benefits of believing in God outweigh the costs (which I do not grant), the crucial point is belief. Of course we can freely decide to engage in religious *practices* if we decide to do so, but can we adopt *beliefs* just because we want to do so? That is, can you make yourself believe a proposition p that you do not now believe because you see that it is in your interest to do so? Surely not.[18]

## Attempts to Discredit Religion

Thus far our results are relatively innocuous. While the broad phenomenon of religious belief—that is, the truth of (1)—may be largely explainable in cognitive or evolutionary terms, actual religions (e.g., Christianity) cannot. This is because (so I argue) commitment to them is too costly. I say this point is relatively innocuous because CSR proponents recognize that actual religions are costly and are products not just of evolution but of evolution plus culture.

But many religious skeptics, some of whom are involved in CSR, try to discredit religious beliefs in various ways. Several different arguments can be found in the literature. Here are four of them, together with responses.[19]

First, the most common argument is this: religious beliefs are pointless and otiose because we can give perfectly good explanations of why people hold them—explanations that do not posit any God or gods or supernatural forces. There is no need to appeal to religious explanations of GRB or FBRB; they are redundant. Thus Matthew Alper agues as follows: "If belief in God is produced by a genetically inherited trait, if the human species is 'hardwired' to believe in a spirit world, this could suggest that God doesn't exist as something 'out there,' beyond and independent of us."[20]

It is a good question whether we can give adequate naturalistic, perhaps evolutionary, explanations of religion.[21] But suppose we can do so or come close to doing so. Alper claims that this "could suggest" atheism, and I suppose he is right that it *could* do so. But *would* it do so, or (more importantly) would it *entail* atheism or even make atheism more probable than it was before? Of course not. This is because we have not ruled out the possibility that God does exist and uses natural causes and mechanisms to make people conscious of God. Perhaps God intentionally created human beings with cognitive equipment and mechanisms that help bring about religious beliefs. In general, it is a fallacy (the genetic fallacy) to suppose that explaining the origin of a belief refutes that belief.[22]

Second, religious beliefs are examples of wishful thinking, which we can define as believing that something is true not because of evidence that it is true but because of a desire that it be true. Thus, we would like there to exist a loving heavenly Father who protects us, rewards us and grants us eternal bliss after death, and so we believe that such a being exists.

But when we look at the actual requirements of most religions, the concept of wish fulfillment at play in this second antireligious argument has to get stretched all out of recognition to make it fit. As noted earlier, the truth is that many religions are costly and difficult; they make extreme demands on people's behavior. Of course people can claim to be religious and yet live in self-serving and hedonistic ways. Most religions would hardly recognize such folks as genuinely religious. But even if this is so, the religious critic has another suggestion: perhaps, in a twisted way, we *want* to be punished, to practice asceticism, to feel pain, to work extraordinarily hard to atone for our sins, to suffer for our faith and so on. But such a claim is implausible in the extreme. There probably are some religious folk who suffer from some such pathology, but it is obvious that few religious people have these sorts of masochistic impulses.

Moreover, if religious belief is a product of wish fulfillment, why is this not true of religious nonbelief? Perhaps the absence of belief is the result of a desire to see the universe as a godless place. Perhaps many atheists do not believe in God because, like Nagel (see endnote 16), they do not want God to exist.

Third, the processes and mechanisms that produce religious beliefs are unreliable because they cause people to form beliefs that cannot possibly be verified or falsified (e.g., "God exists" or "There is life after death").

Some religious beliefs are indeed unfalsifiable, but that can hardly count as an indictment of all of them. There are unfalsifiable beliefs in every area of life, even in science (e.g., the belief that natural laws will hold in the future just as they have in the past). Atheists too hold unfalsifiable beliefs (e.g., the belief that there is no conscious life beyond death).

Fourth, those same processes and mechanisms are unreliable because they produce inconsistent beliefs. For example, Muslims hold that there exists one and only one God; many Hindus hold that there are many gods; and some Buddhists hold that there is no God.

But it may be that a belief in a supernatural reality of some sort (which virtually all religions share) is a true belief but that the ways that belief gets spelled out in the various religions cannot all be true. In other words, the basic religious impulse, unformed and inchoate as it is, is reliable, but the various ways people and cultures interpret it may not be. What this argument shows at most is that there are different interpretations of divine reality (which I would have thought we knew already); it does not show that there is no divine reality.

Of course, if we knew ahead of time that the mechanisms that produce religious belief are systematically unreliable, some of these criticisms might be cogent. But we do not know this. Or if we knew ahead of time that God does not exist or that some robust version of naturalism is true, some or all of these criticisms might be cogent.[23] But we do not know ahead of time that God does not exist or that naturalism is true.

Philosophers distinguish between two sorts of defeaters of claims or arguments. A *rebutting defeater* amounts to a refutation of the claim or argument. It would seem odd to me for anyone to think that the arguments we have discussed constitute refutations of GRB or of any version of FBRB. But do these arguments, or any of them, amount to *undercutting defeaters*? Such a defeater, if successful, removes the grounds for the belief; it shows that it is not rational to make the claim or endorse the argument in question.

As we have seen, explanations of why someone believes something never amount to rebutting defeaters of the belief. But such explanations can count as undercutting defeaters. Suppose I believe that I will soon be extraordinarily wealthy because I will win the lottery. And suppose the reason I have that belief is that I read a message to that effect in my tea leaves this morning. That would not show that my belief is false (I might in fact win the lottery), but it would show that my belief is irrational. So is it possible that causal explanations of GRB and FBRB given by CSR amount to undercutting defeaters of those beliefs? Do they show that it is irrational to believe in GRB or FBRB?

It seems to me that the answer is no. Again, if we knew that no supernatural beings exist, the answer might well be yes, but we do not know this. Or if the theist had no other reason to believe in God besides the tendency described in the first argument, the answer again might be yes. But theists typically do have other reasons; preeminently, they have what they take to be their own (and others') experience of God. In the tea leaves case, we know that the causal factors producing the belief are unreliable, and we know that the future winning of the lottery was not itself causally involved in the production of the belief. But we do not know that God was not involved in the production of the theist's belief in God or that the mechanisms that produced belief in God are unreliable.

## Christian Belief as Appropriate

As a Christian myself, I hold that Christian belief is natural in the sense of appropriate. Although I am unable to prove the point, there are two central reasons. First, I believe one result of recent philosophical discussions about religion is that religious believers, in their apologetic efforts, have largely defended their views well in response to the objections of critics of religion. They have not proved Christianity or even theism to be true, of course, but in my view they have plausibly replied to all the putative defeaters I am aware of. Moreover, although all these next points can be (and are) debated, it seems to me that there are certain facts about our world that atheists at the very least have to work hard to account for. For example, the fact that there is anything at all as opposed to nothing, the fact that the universe is intelligible, the existence of objective moral facts, the "fine-tuning" of the universe for life and the existence of consciousness.[24] Obviously, I cannot substantiate these points here.

Second, I accept the claim that religious beliefs and practices are largely the result of experienced human needs. It's just that I think those needs are God-given. As Augustine famously prayed, "You have made us for yourself, and our hearts are restless until they repose in thee."[25]

Specifically what needs am I talking about? I think the following points (noted already) about human wants and needs are part of what we might call "the human condition": (1) we want to understand our place as human beings in the universe; (2) we want to escape, to the degree possible, from misfortune and suffering for ourselves and our loved ones; (3) we want to assuage our sense of guilt for wrongdoing; (4) we want to find some sort of overarching meaning in our lives; (5) we want to live as fruitfully and abundantly as possible in some sort of loving and supporting community; and (6) we want to be assured of some sort of life beyond death. Different people feel these needs in different ways, of course, and would rate their importance differently. But to have such needs is, as I say, part of the human condition. And religion is one response to these needs.

So, is *religious belief* natural? My answer is yes and no. The tendency of human beings to believe in some sort of God, gods or supernatural beings can to a great extent be explained along cognitive or evolutionary lines. But as already noted (see endnote 21), I do not believe any such explanation can be complete without adding the point that God created us with a certain need and desire for fellowship with God. Is *Christian belief* natural? In the third sense of *natural*—natural as appropriate, rational—as a Christian myself I affirm that the answer is yes. But is Christian belief natural in the first two senses? I say no. It is far too costly.[26]

# 7

# IS CHRISTIANITY UNIQUE?

In this chapter I want to do three main things.[1] First, I want to raise the fact of religious diversity and discuss various approaches to it. Second, I want to criticize one such approach—namely, religious pluralism. Third, I want to argue that Christianity is unique among the religions of the world in striking and important ways.

In this chapter, as indeed in the entire book, I am addressing two sorts of people. First, I am speaking to my fellow Christians, trying to show them how we ought to think on the topic of Christianity and the other religions. But I also speak to those who do not see themselves as Christians. I am trying to show them that there is good reason to consider Christianity unique.

## Imagining Religion

I will first return to a point made briefly in chapter six. Here is a thought experiment. Suppose we could go back to the Pleistocene Era, a million years ago or so, and restart the evolution of human knowledge and culture. And suppose further that God, if God exists, never revealed to human beings anything about religion or how they should live. Suppose, that is, that human beings were required, as best they could, to come up with their own religious ideas and practices. Now, my question is, What sorts of religions, in broad outline, might they produce?

I suspect some people might tend toward some version of *legalism*. That is, they would suggest a set of laws or rules, and the idea would be that God or the gods will approve of them or take them to a happy place after death if they obey those laws. Others might tend toward what we can call *ritualism*. That is, they would come up with an elaborate set of rites or rituals and suggest that God or the gods will be appeased and will cause things to go well for them if they perform the correct rituals correctly. Some might suggest what we might call *a psychological understanding of religion*. What they need to do, by whatever means—meditation, prayer, peyote—is to get into the right psychological or spiritual state. If they do get into the required enlightened state of mind, they will be tranquil and serene despite the challenges of life. Some might even suggest a version of *relativism*. As long as people are sincerely following the mores of their community or the dictates of their own conscience, God or the gods will protect them.

I will return to these imagined religious impulses later.

## Religious Diversity: Three Views

So the first question I want to ask is, How should Christians understand the other religions? What various approaches are available here? The question is important, among other things, because of two obvious facts: (1) there are impressive and saintly people who belong to religions other than Christianity, and (2) the beliefs of such people seem to be held with intellectual honesty and sincerity.

We cannot just say, in order to be maximally generous, that all the religions are true. Why not? Well, because truth claims are made in all religions (some of the claims are historical, some metaphysical, some ethical), and frequently the truth claims made in one religion are logically incompatible with truth claims made in other religions. For example:

- Some religions claim that there is one and only one God; others hold that there are many gods; many Buddhists claim that there is no God.

- Most Hindus and Buddhists believe in reincarnation, while Christians believe in resurrection.

- Christians believe that ultimate reality (which they call God) is personal in nature, while Advaita Vedanta Hindus affirm that ultimate reality (which they call Brahman) is impersonal.

So which claims are true? Of course religions do not consist merely of truth claims. There are different practices, liturgies, moral commands, sacred texts, dietary regulations, systems of religious organization and so on. But we cannot sensibly deny the fact that the crucial claims of the various religions cannot all be true. And so perhaps the most important question we can ask about a religion is whether its crucial claims are true.

So let's say that a true religion is one whose crucial claims are true. Its diagnosis of the human condition is accurate and its proposed solution really works. And let's say that a false religion is one in which many or all of its crucial truth claims are false. Is there, then, such a thing as a true religion? Should Christians simply say that their religion, Christianity, is true and that all the others are false? Or just what should Christians say?

Three main theological options are available on this point: exclusivism, inclusivism and pluralism.[2] *Exclusivists* in effect say, "My religion is the one and only true way, and those who disagree with it are mistaken." (So far as I can tell, the vast majority of adherents of virtually all the various religions of the world are exclusivist in some such sense as this: they claim that their religion is the one and only true way.) Christian exclusivists typically add that salvation is only available via baptism or a conscious decision for Jesus Christ. Christianity is true because it has been revealed by God; the other religions amount to human wisdom on religious matters. All who die as non-Christians must suffer eternal hell. Christians accordingly have an obligation to evangelize adherents of other religions.

*Inclusivists* affirm that their religion is the best way, but they also argue that other religions are partly true and are somehow included in the inclusivists' own religion. Christian inclusivists, for example, typically affirm that salvation is through Jesus Christ, but suggest that people of other religions can be saved without ever having heard of Christ or the church. An underlying unity of all religions, especially on ethical matters, is recognized and emphasized. For example, the great twentieth-century German Jesuit theologian Karl Rahner argued that Christianity recognizes itself as the "absolute religion" that is intended for all human beings. But at least some non-Christian religions, he said, are "lawful religions" that contain truth and spiritual wisdom. There are, Rahner famously affirmed, "anonymous Christians" in other religions who have "implicit faith." They show that faith by their moral action and by their adherence to the truth as they best know it.[3] So Christian inclusivists see great value in other religions but argue that those religions are completed or fulfilled in Christianity.

*Pluralists* say that my own religion is my way or my community's way, but they insist that other religions are equally valid and valuable roads to salvation.[4] No religion, not even mine, can claim absolute superiority. All religions seem to produce saints and spiritually admirable people about equally as well. You can certainly be deeply committed to your own religion—so pluralists say—but no one religion is intrinsically superior to the others. There must be tolerance and honest dialogue between the religions.

The foremost religious pluralist in recent times is undoubtedly John Hick. Before his retirement, he taught for several years in my hometown of Claremont. He became convinced of pluralism in the 1970s and defended it ever since. His *magnum opus* is called *An Interpretation of Religion.*[5] The following is a quick and sketchy outline of Hick's theory.

Hick borrows a distinction from the philosopher Immanuel Kant between *things as they appear to us* (the phenomena) and *things as they are in themselves* (the noumena). Hick says that the various Gods, gods and impersonal absolutes of the world's religions are religious phenomena; that is, they are the way various human beings, given their historical and cultural backgrounds, perceive the religious noumenon. Hick calls the religious noumenon "The Real." He claims that it is virtually beyond all human conception or description. All we know of the Real is that it is the ground or basis of the various religious experiences people have.

Like the blind men feeling different parts of the elephant, the various religions interpret the Real in different ways. But all such ways, says Hick, are equally valid and religiously helpful apprehensions of the Real. None is strictly true. Hick further thinks that all the religions are at bottom seeking the same spiritual goal—moving people from what he calls self-centeredness to reality-centeredness. And so far as Hick is concerned, all the major religions of the world do that task about equally well.

Accordingly, religious people are still allowed to make religious claims. When Muslims claim that Muhammad was God's final prophet, or when Buddhists claim that following the Four Noble Truths can lead to escape from the cycle of life, death and rebirth, they are making, according to Hick, statements that are only true of the Real as those perceivers apprehend the Real. But their statements are not true of the Real itself, which is beyond human knowing.

## Problems with Hick's Pluralism

There are many points that I could raise against pluralism. I will mention three.

*1. Religious people will fail to recognize their own religion here.* In some ways it is unfair to say that in Hick's description of religion, religious people will fail to recognize their own religion. For Hick and other pluralists aim not to propose a new religion but to offer a theory in the philosophy of religion. Nevertheless, pluralism appears to have religious implications; it does not quite leave the religions untouched. I am not thinking so much of the fact that most people in most religions are in some sense exclusivists and so will reject any version of pluralism. My point is more like this: suppose that as a Christian I want to affirm the statement *God created the heavens and the earth*. Hick's theory of course allows me as a Christian to make that statement; still, it is undeniable that Hick's pluralism entails that the statement is false. Indeed, virtually any truth claim made in any religion will have to be considered false, on Hick's theory. And, as I say, most religious people will want to resist that conclusion. So my point is that Hick's theory will not be greeted warmly by most religious people. What his theory must say about the vast majority of religious beliefs—that they are strictly false—is just what the atheists and naturalists have been saying all along.

Hick's pluralism comes to us in the guise of a purely descriptive theory about religion, but it is clearly prescriptive as well. In effect, it calls for a liberal theological revolution in the religions. On troublesome beliefs like the Christian belief that *Jesus is the incarnate Son of God*, Hick's theory is reductive. It does not allow Christians to hold that that statement is literally true; it is only true of the Real as apprehended by Christians; it is only (as Hick explicitly says) mythologically or metaphorically true.[6] I suspect most Christians will judge this result to be an evisceration of their religion rather than a way of respecting it. This is obviously because Christians, like virtually all religious people, are trying to make true statements about reality.

**2. Do the religions all have a common soteriological aim?** It is true that all the religions in one way or another try to address the fact that human beings are not in the optimal moral or spiritual state, and all propose some sort of recipe for moving people toward that state. But Hick goes much further. He holds that the soteriological aim of all the religions is the same: it is to move people from a state of ego-centeredness to a state of reality-centeredness, which Hick calls salvation/liberation. And this claim seems to me to be simply false. It amounts to what might be called "least common denominator religion." The Zen view of *satori* and the Advaita Vedanta notion of *moksha* seem to me quite unlike each other and even more unlike the Christian notion of reconciliation with God.

**3. Why should we believe Hick's theory?** Suppose that some overenthusiastic and sophomoric Kantian were to claim that (1) my desktop computer (located on my desk in my office in Kravis Center, Claremont McKenna College) and (2) the Grand Canyon in Arizona are two different phenomenological apprehensions of the same, one noumenal reality. I presume that everyone will admit that this thesis has little to commend itself to us. The two items mentioned are far too different from each other for any such thesis to make any sense. There is no reason to believe the thesis, and there are compelling reasons to reject it.

But it seems to me that (1) the Christian God and, say, (2) the Taoist notion of the Tao are also far too different from each other for such a thesis—which Hick is in effect defending—to make any sense. Indeed, I suspect that they are *far more different from each other* than my computer and the Grand Canyon are different from each other. Of course, if someone were to claim that the God of Christianity and the God of Judaism are the same, that thesis might make sense despite some obvious differences (e.g., the fact that Christians hold and Jews deny that God is a Trinity). This is because there is a clear historical connection between the two; Christians have always held that their God is the same God as the God of the Hebrew Bible.

What, then, is the evidence that Hick's thesis is true? So far as I can see, the evidence *against* it is overwhelming. The only evidence in its favor (if evidence is the right word) is a strong desire on the part of pluralists that it be true in order to avoid exclusivism. In some sense I suppose it is trivially true that all the religions represent different responses to the transcendent. But admitting that much does not go very far in validating pluralism.

Accordingly, I claim that pluralism is not the right way to look at the problem of religious diversity.

## A Different Suggestion

So if, as I claim, pluralism is wrong, it is time for me to develop my own stance on these matters. I begin with the thought that Christians do not have a monopoly on religious truth. Christians should admire the spiritual wisdom and insight found in other religions and the saintly adherents of other religions. Moreover, we can learn from other religions. I reject the idea that all the truth worth knowing is found in Christianity and that the other religions are not worth studying. I myself have benefited from exposure to the religions, particularly from Jews I have known and Jewish texts I have read. Moreover, Christians must repent of the imperialistic attitudes that many Christians have or have had. Christian triumphalism—allied, as it often has been, with a sense of American or Western superiority—has manifested itself in some extremely ugly ways in the past and probably continues to do so.

I believe that God loves all people—Christian and non-Christian alike—that God reaches out to all people, and that the Holy Spirit works in other contexts than the Christian church. (As Paul argued in Romans 1–2, no one is totally ignorant of God; some truths about God are "written in our hearts.") So we must treat people of other religions with respect and dignity. I will speak of evangelism later; I will just say here that Christian methods of evangelism must never be coercive or manipulative or even discourteous. We must allow people to practice their own religion freely and without interference. And we must stand shoulder to shoulder with adherents of other religions in efforts to promote justice in the world.

I also believe that our current world badly needs tolerance and acceptance between the religions. So I would highlight the need for dialogue between members of the various religions. Dialogue requires, I believe, three things: honesty, intellectual curiosity and willingness to learn. *Honesty* in religious dialogue means saying what you think is true in your own position and false in your partner's position without subterfuge or evasion. It also means openly admitting difficulties in one's own position and strengths in your partner's position. *Intellectual curiosity* means a desire to learn what your partner sincerely believes, especially when it differs from what you believe. *Willingness to learn* means genuinely wanting to learn about the other religions and allowing previously unrecognized truth to emerge in the process of dialogue itself.

But there are two issues on the general topic of religious disagreement where pluralists and I part company. First, they hold that the mere fact that some people disagree with you on religious topics ought to make you doubt your own beliefs or at least make

you retreat from an exclusivistic stance. But I do not think that
follows at all. As Timothy O'Connor points out, the principle
apparently at work here ought to make pluralists question their
commitment to pluralism, since very many people disagree with
that theory.[7] Of course I do think religious people should avoid
dogmatic narrow-mindedness, but that is another matter.

Second, I think pluralists hold that religious disagreement is
the deepest problem in this area, and that if a plausible pluralistic
theory could be found, those disagreements could be made to go
away and a harmonious world community might ensue. Well, I
too desperately hope for global cooperation, mutual understanding
and trust among people. But why say such a result can only be
achieved on the basis of religious agreement? I would have
thought that something like the reverse is true. The only way that
people of various religions and cultures can come to understand
and cooperate with one another is honestly to recognize their
differences. Minimizing them or subsuming them under some
unifying theory is not the way forward.

So as a Christian I believe both that the supreme revelation of
God to human beings is Jesus Christ, and that people are
reconciled to God through Christ. I further believe that anybody
who disagrees with these claims is mistaken. But I insist that there
is no necessary connection between (1) holding that Christianity
is true and other religions false, and (2) treating people of other
religions in disrespectful ways. It is possible to be a tolerant,
nonimperialist exclusivist.

The *locus classicus* of Christian exclusivism is John 14:6, where
Jesus says, "I am the way, and the truth, and the life. No one comes
to the Father except through me." I agree with this statement.
Salvation, I believe, is found only in him. That is why I reject the
pluralist idea that the other religions are equally good paths to
salvation. Anyone who has ever been reconciled to God or justified

in God's eyes or saved is saved, I believe, only through the life, death and resurrection of Jesus Christ. I do not agree that all religions are equally valid and valuable paths to salvation, nor do I think that Christ is just one among many lords, saviors, prophets and gurus in the religions of the world. Jesus Christ is the incarnate Son of God. He is, as the villagers of Sychar in John 4 said, "the Savior of the world."

So must all non-Christians then go to hell? That is the question critics always ask at this point. And in truth it is both a good question and something of a red herring. Few Christians in the history of theology have insisted that all non-Christians must end up in hell. What about Old Testament saints like Abraham or Ruth or Jeremiah or Daniel? Haven't we always thought that we would see them in the kingdom of God? And isn't it absurd to think that they were Christians? Or what about people who lived and died in the interior of Borneo five thousand years ago? Must they be condemned to hell because they were never baptized or believed in Christ?

Of course not. I have never thought that idea made any sense, nor do most exclusivists. I believe that through the grace and mercy of God some way unknown to us is provided for them. There is insufficient material in Scripture or in Christian tradition to provide us with clear direction here. We cannot dogmatize. We do not know how God reaches and judges such folk. Some suggest that they can be saved on the basis of the best that they know about God and the moral life. Others suggest that they can be saved by a sincere desire and intention to be righteous. Still others suggest that they are given a chance after death to hear and respond to God's good news. (At this point I believe that C. S. Lewis's book *The Great Divorce* has been a helpful myth for many Christians.) I myself have tentatively argued for this third option, but I do not push it as the only available or best alternative.[8] All we know is that God loves all persons and wants all persons to be saved (1 Timothy 2:4), and that God is a God of justice. That is enough for me. I trust that God will be fair.

So on the topic of religious diversity and Christian attitudes toward it, how then can we distinguish between theories that ought to be acceptable to the Christian community and those that are not? My criterion is a practical rather than a theoretical one—it is *evangelism*.[9] My claim then is this: any theory that in effect minimizes, belittles, discourages or rules out evangelism is to be rejected. In my view, all versions of religious pluralism and many versions of inclusivism do just that. We sever the vital nerve of Christian faith when we feel no urgent need to share the good news with people and convert them, if possible, to Christ. As Jesus said in what we call the Great Commission (Matthew 28:19): "Go therefore and make disciples of all nations."

Exclusivists are sometimes accused of being arbitrary in picking out *their* religion, among all the others, as the true religion. They are also sometimes said to be arrogant in doing so. But the arbitrariness objection can only stick if it be granted that all the religions are epistemologically and evidentially on a par. I am unwilling to grant that point. I believe that a decisive noncircular case can be made in favor of many crucial Christian claims. As for arrogance, it is hard to see why Christian exclusivists are any more arrogant than the pluralists themselves. Both hold that their own point of view is true and that all theories inconsistent with it are false. Moreover, if crucial Christian claims are true—for example, *we are all sinners and need to ask God for forgiveness*—the best thing that Christians can do for people, both religious skeptics and adherents of other religions, is tell them the truth.

Let me make something of a confession: *I am not existentially interested in the religions of the world.* I am of course intellectually and academically interested in them. I have always been personally curious about them. And I think the world badly needs understanding and tolerance among the religions. But I am not interested in them existentially (i.e., relative to my own spiritual enlightenment and well being). As a longtime teacher of ancient philosophy, I can use this analogy: I admire the religions of the world much as I admire, enjoy and respect the philosophy of Plato. I look neither to Plato nor to the religions to solve life's deepest puzzles or to provide answers to our spiritual problems. Those answers, I believe, are to be found in Christ.

## Christian Uniqueness

So I turn to the third issue that I want to consider. Is Christianity unique among the religions of the world?

There are, of course, many senses in which Christianity is not unique. It is one of the major religions of the world, along with the others like Hinduism, Buddhism, Judaism, Islam and the like. Moreover, as many people have pointed out, the great religions all agree, to an amazing degree, on ethical and moral matters. Christians will not be surprised by this fact. Paul argues in Romans 1–2 that God has implanted within all human beings a sense of moral responsibility and a rough-and-ready sense of what is morally right and morally wrong. Whether we follow that sense and obey our own moral notions is of course a separate issue.

Moreover, all the religions are unique in some senses. No religion besides Judaism has a holiday called Yom Kippur; no religion other than Islam observes Ramadan. But I want to argue that Christianity is unique in a far more fundamental sense. I will push the argument in three ways. The first has to do with history; the second has to do with the notion of grace; and the third has to do with the founder of Christianity.

However, I first need to point out two limitations of my argument. First, I am not claiming that nothing like these three points can be found elsewhere than in Christianity. I am arguing that my three points, taken together, are what make Christianity unique. Second, I must note that even if I am correct in what I will claim (i.e., even if Christianity is unique in these or other ways), that by itself does not necessarily mean that Christianity is true. As a Christian myself, I naturally believe that it is true, but I want to point out that I will not have tried to show that in this chapter.

*1. The importance of history.* Although my first point does not make Christianity absolutely unique among the religions, it certainly comes close. The truth of Christianity depends importantly on certain events that it claims occurred in history. In the case of most religions, what matters is the content of the religious teachings found in their sacred books or the words of their founders. What importantly matters to Hindus are the teachings found in the *Bhagavad Gita* or other sacred texts, not any historical events. Even in Islam, where historical claims about the life of Muhammad are certainly made, what really matters is the text itself, what was revealed to him. In principle, God could have revealed the Qur'an to somebody else at another time and place.

Here is an event that I remember discussing when I was a student at Princeton Theological Seminary years ago. It concerns Buddhism. Late in his career, the great Protestant theologian Paul Tillich traveled to Japan. He asked some Buddhist scholars in Kyoto this question, "If some historian should make it probable that a man of the name Gautama never lived, what would be the consequence for Buddhism?" The Buddhist scholars replied by denying that the historicity of the Buddha was an issue for Buddhists. "According to the doctrine of Buddhism, the *dharma kaya* [the body of truth] is eternal, and so it does not depend on the history of Gautama."[10] So it does not crucially matter whether

Gautama the Buddha said and did what Buddhists typically say he said and did, or even whether he really existed. Those issues do not affect the truth of Buddhist teachings, which are what really matter.

But Christianity stands or falls on the basis of certain historical claims, preeminently that a man named Jesus lived, died and rose from the dead. At one level this creates a problem for Christianity—unlike most religions, it potentially can be falsified by historical evidence. If it could be proved, for example, that Jesus never lived or that he did not rise from the dead, then Christianity would be in big trouble. Christian faith is intrinsically grounded in the person and history of Jesus of Nazareth. Accordingly, Christianity is not essentially a collection of teachings that can be detached from the deliverer of those teachings. It is essentially based on key historical events in which—so Christians believe—God decisively intervened in human history. One such crucial event is Jesus' resurrection from the dead, which Paul explicitly says Christianity cannot do without (1 Corinthians 15:14-19).

*2. The uniqueness of grace.* As to my second point on the uniqueness of Christianity, please recall our thought experiment at the outset of this chapter about what sorts of religious ideas human beings might come up with on their own. All of them have something important in common: they all recognize, quite rightly, that something is deeply wrong about the human condition, and they all propose a solution. But the point that is most interesting to me is that they all suggest solutions that human beings are capable of achieving. If you try hard enough, you *can* obey the laws. If you have learned them and are diligent, you *can* practice the correct rituals correctly. If you go through the proper spiritual exercises, you *can* achieve an enlightened state of mind. The message to humans, then, is that the path may be difficult, even extremely difficult, but *you can do you it.*

Here then is one point where Christianity is unique: Christianity insists that human beings are not capable of saving themselves. The essential problem in human life is not false consciousness—that is, failure to understand the religious truth—but guilt. We have sinned against a holy and perfect God, and we deserve to be punished. What God requires of us we are incapable of delivering. Accordingly, if anyone at all is to be saved, God must do the saving. That is the essence of the Christian notion of grace. God rescues us even though we are lost. God loves us even though we are unlovable. God accepts us even though we are unacceptable. God forgives us even though we are unforgivable. Now there are certainly other religions where God or the gods assist us in our spiritual efforts. There is even a notion in Pure Land Buddhism of something that is analogous to grace, but it has more to do with transfer of merit, and so is not the same thing.

Christianity is the only religion that says our terrible spiritual condition—which Christians call sin—deserves punishment from a just and morally good God, and that God paid that penalty himself. And although we cannot earn it, there is something we Christians must do, of course. But it is merely a matter of accepting gratefully what God has already done for us.

*3. The uniqueness of Jesus Christ.* Almost all religions have famous founders (Hinduism is an exception)—people like Moses, the Buddha, Muhammad and Guru Nanak. But Jesus is unlike them in many ways. One important difference is this: most of the great religious founders were essentially teachers or gurus; Jesus Christ (according to Christians) is a savior. Indeed, Christians claim that in Jesus Christ God became a human being. This idea is called the incarnation. God became a human, so Christians hold, to show us what God is like and to make it possible for human beings to know God (apart from Christ, people can have only a hazy and inchoate knowledge of God). Moreover, the incarnation and resurrection were designed to defeat all the forces in the world that oppose God's rule—forces like sin, death, suffering and despair.

But why this strange and puzzling claim that Jesus had to be both divine and human? Let's consider each claim. He had to be *human* for three reasons: (1) because pure God in our midst would only dazzle and frighten us; we would not understand what God was trying to say or do; (2) because God wanted to declare as fully as possible his love for us and solidarity with us; the incarnation means that our fate is intimately (rather than remotely) tied to God; and (3) because God cannot die, let alone die on anybody's behalf.

And Jesus Christ had to be *divine* for three reasons: (1) because we human beings are incapable of saving ourselves; if we are to be reconciled to God, then God must accomplish it; (2) because we human beings cannot defeat death; if death is to be overcome, God must do the overcoming; and (3) if Jesus were a mere human being, he would in the end amount to nothing more than a great religious hero like all the others. But if Jesus was indeed God incarnate, there is an undeniable finality about him and his path to God.

If Christianity were a set of ethical or legal rules that human beings, by their own efforts, were capable of satisfying, then we would not need a savior. The same would be true if Christianity were essentially a series of rituals or a set of spiritual exercises. In such cases, a guru would do just fine. Christianity certainly involves an ethic and contains laws, rituals and practices, but at heart it is not any such thing. It is a set of beliefs and deeds that form our feeble response to a surprising and undeserved act of infinite love that God has performed on our behalf.

So I do not accept the idea that Christianity and the other religions are on an epistemic or evidential par. Christians recognize many confirming signs of Jesus' status—his intimate relation to God, his authority to forgive sins, his call for belief in him. But the central sign for the church has always been Jesus' resurrection from the dead (see chap. 4). Now in the history of the world, other people besides Jesus have apparently been raised from the dead—some of them even in the context of other religions. I think that is quite possible; I have no problem with the idea that God can work miraculously in other contexts than the Christian context. (Naturally, that does not necessarily mean that I accept all such claims.) But like Lazarus in the Bible, or like certain extraordinarily fortunate people in hospitals these day, these people were resuscitated; they were restored to their old manner of life, only inevitably to die a second time at some later point, this time presumably for good. Christ was not resuscitated but resurrected; he was raised to a new level of life; he was transformed into what Paul called a glorified body; he still lives today. The resurrection of Jesus from the dead was a graphic way for God to repeat what God had said about Jesus at his baptism: "This is my beloved Son, the Beloved, with whom I am well pleased" (Matthew 3:17).[11]

There are many views of Jesus Christ in the world today. Muslims honor Jesus as a great prophet, but the Qur'an denies the resurrection by insisting that Jesus did not really die on the cross. Some revisionist Christians like John Hick see Jesus as essentially a great teacher, acutely conscious of the presence of God in his life, but not the incarnate Son of God. I respect the right of Muslims to have their own beliefs about Jesus or about anything else. And I do not question the integrity of people like Hick who disagree with my Christology. But I reserve the right to argue against views of Jesus that I consider wrong or unhelpful to the Christian community. Jesus Christ is Lord. Jesus Christ is the way to God.[12]

In the New Testament a connection is made between Jesus' resurrection from the dead and his status as Son of God (see Romans 1:3-4). We live in a world in which messiahs, gurus and holy people proliferate. In such a world, how can we know who to follow? Which messiah is the true messiah? Paul's answer (through Luke) to the Athenian philosophers on Mars Hill was that Jesus is the man who God has appointed and "of this he has given assurance to all by raising him from the dead" (Acts 17:31). Many messiahs have commanding personalities. Many gurus are full of spiritual wisdom. Many holy people recommend noble lifestyles. But none of them was resurrected from the dead.

I believe that if Jesus had not been raised, Christianity would not exist today. He would have ended up a fine teacher of religion and ethics—like Socrates or Gandhi, perhaps—but not the Savior of the world. I believe the resurrection was God's way of pointing to Jesus and saying, *He* is the one you are to follow. *He* is the Savior. *He* is Lord.

# DO EVIL AND SUFFERING SHOW THAT GOD DOES NOT EXIST?

The problem of evil is probably the foremost intellectual difficulty that theists face. If God is all-powerful, all-knowing and perfectly good, why is there so much undeserved and needless suffering? Surely, if God is all-powerful, God has the ability to prevent needless suffering. And surely, if God is perfectly good, God would not want there to be needless suffering. Since, as it clearly seems, there is needless suffering, either God is not all-powerful or is not perfectly good, or else does not exist. Many proposed solutions to the problem have been considered over the centuries, and the debate continues unabated to this day.

Let us define the word *evil* in a rough-and-ready way. We will simply call it *undeserved human suffering*. I actually believe that the category of evil is broader than this; it is sometimes evil when animals suffer, for example, and it is possible to do evil that does not cause any suffering at all. But for our purposes we can ignore these complications. Undeserved human suffering might be caused by another human being or group of human beings, or by natural, nonhuman causes like earthquakes, hurricanes, diseases and famines. Following current usage, we can call the first "moral evil" and the second "natural evil."

The word *theodicy* was invented by the poet Milton. He defined it as a "defense of the ways of God to man." We now use the word to refer to any response to the problem of evil and suffering in the world that defends religious faith. Following Alvin Plantinga, philosophers now distinguish between a theodicy and a defense.[1] A *defense* tries merely to suggest what God's reasons might possibly be for permitting evil. This strategy, as Plantinga suggests, can be sufficient to rebut the common claim that theists contradict themselves in believing that God is all-powerful, that God is perfectly good and that evil exists. A *theodicy* tries to give God's actual reasons for permitting evil. My argument in this chapter amounts to a theodicy.[2]

## God's Aims in Creation

I believe that the problem of evil can best be solved given theological assumptions that Christians are prepared to make and nonbelievers are not.[3] Most of the assumptions that I have in mind concern Christ and the future. I also agree with Marilyn Adams that what she calls "horrors" have to be dealt with in theodicy,[4] that God can use human suffering in the ways she suggests, that any solution to the problem of evil must crucially involve the eschaton and that intimacy with God is the highest human good.

In my view, God had three great aims in creation. First, God wanted to create a world that contained that greatest possible balance of moral and natural good over moral and natural evil. Second, God wanted to do so given a world in which human beings were free (in what philosophers call a libertarian sense of freedom) to say yes or no to God, to obey or disobey God, to love or hate God. Third, the first two entail that what God wanted was a world in which as many human beings as possible would freely say yes to God and accept God's salvation. Free will theodicies always say, following Augustine, that the existence of moral evil is not God's fault (at least not directly); it is ours. But of course the point must be immediately added that God is indirectly responsible in that God created the overall situation in which humans are free and moral evils are possible. And, most unfortunately, moral evil is just what human beings freely decide to do much of the time.

Why then did God create free moral agents in the first place? In the light of all the evil that we see in the world, have not God's overall plans been thwarted? Not so, I say. God's policy decision to make human beings free was wise, for it will turn out better in the long run that we act freely, even if we sometimes err, than it would have turned out had we been created as innocent automata, programmed always to do good. The good that will result in the end will far outweigh the evil. The enormous favorable balance of good over evil that will then exist, given the great good of the eschaton, was obtainable by God in no other way or in no other morally preferable way.

Christians believe that in the end God will outsmart us and bring limitless good out of evil, as God did in the cross of Christ. That is, out of a terrible injustice, God brought about the great good of our salvation (1 Peter 3:18). Christians also believe that despite the evils of this life, in the end God will be glorified. Crucifixion was a sign of shame and ignominy; now the cross has become the central symbol of the Christian faith: "For our sake he made him to be sin who knew no sin, so that in him we might become the righteousness of God" (2 Corinthians 5:21). God is stronger than all the forces of pain and evil; God will win in the end.

What then do we say to sufferers or to sufferers of horrendous evils? I want to say two things. First, suffering, and the waiting that it almost always includes, can be spiritually uplifting. Certainly pain does not always help people rise to new moral and spiritual heights—sometimes it destroys personality. But it can produce spiritual good: it can be a stimulus to spiritual growth and to trust in God more fully. When we suffer we are often vulnerable and malleable, so suffering can be a kind of wake-up call to the effect that we need to grow spiritually.[5]

Second, God is with us in our suffering, loving us and caring for us. I take it that this is the lesson of Paul's eloquent outburst in Romans 8:

> If God is for us, who is against us? He who did not withhold his own Son, but gave him up for all of us, will he not with him also give us everything else? Who will bring any charge against God's elect? It is God who justifies. Who is to condemn? . . . Who will separate us from the love of Christ? (Romans 8:31-35)

Paul concludes on the ringing note that nothing—and that includes all human pains, fears and experiences of horrendous evil—"will be able to separate us from the love of God in Christ Jesus our Lord" (Romans 8:39).

But what about natural evil? Briefly, it seems that given God's aims in creation, creating a world that is regular and lawlike (i.e., a world with a coherent system of natural causes and effects) is in God's interests. In such a world, natural events can in principle (though not always in fact) be understood, explained and even predicted. Some of those events will be good and some bad (in the sense of causing undeserved human suffering). It is, in short, in God's interests to create a world in which pain occurs and sometimes results from natural causes. Divine interventions in the world to bring about good things or prevent bad things must be rare. Most of the time God must stay out of the way and let the natural world take its course. Otherwise, the world would be highly irregular and unpredictable.

One way to grasp this point is to imagine a world in which human beings suffer no pain—that is, in which human experience is only pleasurable and we are at all times blissfully happy. I briefly mentioned this point in chapter two; let's call this a "valium world." In such a world, the results would be disastrous from God's point of view. There would be little or no sense of morality, of some things being good and others evil. There would be little sense that our decisions and actions have consequences. There would be no compassion for others or occasion to help others. There would be no courage or heroism. There would be no reason for moral growth or improving one's soul. There would be no spiritual longing for moral excellence or for a better world. There would be little felt reason to love and obey God. There would be no growth through suffering. So it seems that there are certain great goods that God can only or best achieve by allowing natural evil.

An objection: But then why is *natural* evil required? Could not moral evil alone have accomplished the same purposes? There is some truth here: it seems that morality could exist, as well as a sense that our actions have consequences, in a world of no natural evil. Compassion and courage could exist. But the answer to the objection is that a world of moral evil alone would still not have sufficed for God's purposes. This is because in a world in which the only evil is moral evil, most human beings would not learn the requisite moral and spiritual lessons; we would spend our time blaming the perpetrators of moral evil and trying to exact revenge on them. Natural evil means that there is human suffering that we cannot blame on other human beings. Without it, there would still be a deficit in the human longing for moral growth and unity with God.

The divine desires for the world noted previously necessitated certain criteria that the world has to satisfy. (1) It has to be an environment in which God's existence and desires for us, and the long-term consequences of the moral and religious choices that humans would make, would not be obvious to us. God must be slightly hidden; there must be (to borrow John Hick's term) a certain "epistemic distance" between human beings and God. (2) It has to be a world in which rewards do not immediately follow from behaving in ways approved by God and punishments do not immediately follow from behaving in ways disapproved by God. (3) It has to be a world in which God's love and grace is at least potentially available (to accept or reject) to all people.

This is why I believe Adams is wrong in accusing "overall balance" and nonuniversalist theodicies of overriding God's desire to be good to all human beings.[6] God is good to all, I say, in offering the gift of God's grace and forgiveness to everyone without exception, either in this life or in the eschaton. There are Christian theologies (e.g., limited atonement theories) that are not able to say as much.

The difference between believers and nonbelievers is not just that Christians believe certain things that non-Christians do not. Another crucial difference is that believers *trust in God*. They believe that God has answers to many questions that now appear unanswerable. Christians believe that God has good reasons for allowing evil to exist. Christians do not always claim to know what those reasons are, but they trust in God nonetheless.

God is transcendent, and we face severe cognitive limits (1 Corinthians 13:12). Accordingly, we should naturally expect there to be evils that we cannot explain but God can, and goods so great that we cannot comprehend them but God can. This Paul exults: "O the depth of the riches and wisdom and knowledge of God! How unsearchable are his judgments and how inscrutable his ways!" (Romans 11:33). So the fact that there are mysteries in theodicy and truths beyond our ken is not a last-ditch attempt to save a Christian theology from criticism but rather exactly what that theology should lead us to expect.

So the problem of evil, although it remains a difficulty and a source of worry for Christians, does not constitute a refutation of theism. The problem can be disarmed as a daunting intellectual objection to Christianity. Some evil will be used by God to produce greater good (either greater earthly goods or the omni-good of the kingdom of God), and all evil will be overcome and transcended in the eschaton. For the redeemed in the kingdom of God, all tears will be wiped away, all diseases will be healed, all crimes will be repented of and forgiven, all injustice will be made right, all questions will be answered, all relationships will be restored, and all suffering will be redeemed.

### Trust in God

Trust in God is not blind trust. The trust that Christians have in God is trust that grows out of their experience (and their community's experience): they have known God's guidance, God's protection, God's forgiveness. Jeremiah, Job and Jesus are all biblical figures who experienced severe difficulties and even agonies. Each in the face of disaster asked God tough questions (and so can we). But each ultimately rested his case and trusted in God (see Job 1:21; 42:1-6; Lamentations 3:21-26; Luke 22:42; 23:46). Christians choose to cast their lot with them.

Do Jesus' teachings say anything to victims of evil? Is it possible to love one's enemy, for example (see Matthew 5:39-41, 43-47; Luke 6:27-28)? Well, it may not be possible by sheer force of will to conjure up in oneself feelings of love for an enemy (or maybe for anyone). But it certainly is possible to decide to act in certain ways: to accept an enemy, to forgive an enemy and to help an enemy. And perhaps behaving in those sorts of ways is what love at its deepest level amounts to. Is it possible to love or forgive someone who has caused you to experience horrendous evil? For some few saintly people, even here and now, it is possible. But in the eschaton, after we have been transformed by the vision of God's face, I believe it will be not only possible but actual.

Jesus' teachings are highly relevant here. He taught about the importance of forgiveness, both human (Matthew 18:21-22) and divine (Luke 23:34), and a supremely excellent eschaton makes no sense unless God has forgiven us of our sins and we have forgiven those who have sinned against us. And Jesus' teachings about future compensation for sufferers will be fulfilled in the eschaton (Mark 10:29-30; Luke 6:21). Union with God is the highest human good.

I agree with Adams that suffering can be incorporated into a larger narrative that involves the sufferer finding God. Indeed, I think human suffering can help lead a person to joy and peace here and now. (Obviously, it does not always do so.) After the glorious and uplifting event that Christians call the transfiguration, Jesus made this shocking announcement to the disciples: "The Son of Man must undergo great suffering, and be rejected by the elders, chief priests, and scribes, and be killed, and on the third day be raised" (Luke 9:22). Maybe we too, like Jesus, have to suffer, some of us horrendously, on our paths toward God. And perhaps we will one day see how everything in our lives was part of our journey to the presence of God. At the end, we too will not "wish it away," as Adams says. For now, it is, as I have argued, a matter of trust in God.

So the basic claim of my approach to the problem of evil is that God will redeem all evil. It will be done two ways: (1) Some evil will be used causally by God to help produce the great good of the kingdom of God. (2) In the kingdom of God all evil will be overcome, transcended, made to pale into insignificance in the light of the infinite good to be revealed there.

## Evil and Hope

I conclude by making a related but different point: the need for God in the light of horrendous evils. My question is this: Is there any sense in which horrendous evils can be a springboard for hope? Or is there room at all for hope in a world where evils abound and horrendous evils occur?

My reply is, *Unless God exists, our grounds for hope in the light of horrendous evil are limited indeed*. If no Creator or higher power such as the God of theism exists, the only hope that we can sensibly have in the light of evil is tenuous. It is the hope that some day we can design our educational, social, political and diplomatic systems in such a way that no more horrendous evils, and far fewer evils, occur. And if horrendous evils are sometimes instances of natural evil, this hope must also involve almost unimaginable medical, scientific and technological progress in controlling nature.

So if God does not exist, a world free of horrendous evils and containing far fewer evils is the best world we can hope for. Those who believe in inevitable human progress will perhaps find this a possible hope. Those, like me, who do not share that belief will reply that we can certainly *hope* for such an outcome, but that it will be something like hope that continental drift will cease. Certainly, if God does not exist, there is no hope whatsoever for any experience of reparation or even joy for those who have experienced horrendous evils and are now dead. They are gone forever. That sort of hope only makes sense if God exists. If one holds that God does not exist, and if one's assessment of human nature (and nature itself) is such that the possibility of horrendous evil can never be ruled out, well, that reasoning seems to me to lead to despair.

Is it possible for evil, and even horrendous evil, to be redeemed? That of course will depend in large part on what we mean by the word *redeem*. If redeeming evil means restoring conditions so that an evil or even horrendously evil event (e.g., African slavery or the Holocaust) never occurred, then obviously no evil can be redeemed. This outcome follows from the metaphysical principle that the past is fixed and unchangeable. It is too late for anyone, even God, to change past facts. Nor can redeeming evil have anything to do with our one day understanding that events such as African slavery or the Holocaust in the long run were actually *good*. Some evils can surely be redeemed in that sense. Probably all human beings have experienced undeserved suffering where they later come to understand that it was for the best that it occurred. But not events of this sort.

Well then, is there any sense in which horrendous evil *can* be redeemed? The answer is yes, but only if God exists. If no God exists, evils, especially horrendous evils, cannot be redeemed at all. But if a perfectly good and all-powerful supreme being exists (as Jews and Christians claim), a sort of redemption is possible. Suppose such a being provides punishment for the perpetrators of horrendous evil and a limitlessly good afterlife for victims of horrendous evil (as well as others, of course) in which their horrific earthly experiences fade further and further away in memory and eventually pale into insignificance in the light of the infinite goodness then revealed and experienced. If that occurs, I think it will amount to something like the redemption of horrendous evil.

Religious skeptics will dismiss talk like this as sheer silliness or wishful thinking. And certainly they are allowed to declare with bravado their credo—that this life is all that there is, that death is the complete end of human beings, and that we had best get used to the idea that we live in a radically unjust world. There simply is no redemption of horrendous evil—so they will insist—or compensation for its victims.

But there is no denying that most human beings have a deep longing for justice and a hope that the world will turn out just. I believe that the reality of horrendous evil in our world for most people increases, rather than decreases, that longing. Wishes do not make things like this come true, of course. But for those of us who want to avoid despair, the sort of hope I have been describing is appealing. For those of us who also believe in God, it is not just a hope but a conviction.

Accordingly, if you are a person of hope, I say that horrendous evils ought to convince you that God exists.

# CAN WE BE HAPPY
# APART FROM GOD?

Actually, the question that forms this chapter's title, "Can we be happy apart from God?" is not quite the question that I want to answer.[1] But I am sometimes asked this and related questions, especially by students. My answer to it would be yes. I know many atheists and agnostics who, so far as I can tell, live happy lives. That is certainly possible. But I want, if I can, to deflect attention away from happiness. So far as I can tell, it is not one of the major goals of Christianity to make people happy, where happiness is understood as a subjective feeling. But something like that often does happen to Christians as a kind of byproduct. We might call it well-being or thriving.

Of course everybody wants to be happy, and I am no exception: I want to be happy. But I would have thought that the major personal goal of Christianity is not to be happy but to honor God in your life.

## The Human Condition

Accordingly, in this chapter I will take a different tack—I want to continue with a point I made very briefly at the end of chapter two. I want to argue that human beings have certain needs—I will speak about five of them—that God can meet. So I do claim that we can be better people, more fulfilled people, maybe even (as a serendipitous byproduct) happier people if we are rightly related to God.

My overall argument has to do with what is often called "the human condition." The point is that human beings have needs they desperately want to be met and questions they desperately want to be answered. These are some of our deepest longings as human beings. And I want to argue that people should be properly related to God because I think that God can meet those needs and provide those answers. Some of the questions that I have in mind, of course, have answers on the assumption of naturalism (some do not), but my point is that I much prefer the answers that are available if theism is true. One more caveat: some of the points I want to make presuppose not just general theism but the Christian God.

## Our Place in the World

The first argument revolves around such questions as Who am I? What is my place in the universe? Why do I exist? Is there any purpose or meaning to my life? What sort of world do I live in? Is it a world created by God, or what? What is the best way for me to live? I think all human beings—or all reflective ones, anyway—ask those sorts of questions. And God, if God exists and if you listen to God, can answer them. Apart from God, there are few available answers to those questions, and we will be in a state of ignorance and confusion. People can accordingly experience alienation from their world and from themselves.

If God exists, we are creations of God; we might even say children of God. That's who we are. And the purpose of human life is to live in such a way as to honor God and serve humanity as best we can. That is why we are here. Now, nonbelievers will of course deny that those claims are true. But if God exists and reveals his desires to humans, I say we've got access to answers to some of our deepest questions.

As noted, on some of these questions, atheists and agnostics think they know their answers with as much certainty as religious people have. Take the question Is there any purpose to our lives? If *purpose* here means "transcendent purpose," religious skeptics hold that the answer is no. Or take Why do I exist? They would that say we exist because evolution produced us, and that's all there is to it.

Still, if God exists and if God reveals himself to us, we can know our place in the world and the purpose of our existence. That is a human need God can satisfy.

## Does My Life Matter?

This leads immediately to the second point: I think we human beings long for a universe in which we matter. Suppose that we live in a godless universe, as atheists believe. Then whether we live or die, whether we suffer or enjoy ourselves, whether our children succeed in life or fail—those things do not ultimately matter. They matter no more in the overall scheme of things than one tadpole in a pond living or dying, or one small stone being crushed by a glacier. As Meursault says in Camus's *The Stranger*, "Nothing, nothing matters."[2] But if God exists, we do matter because God created us and loves us. My life is not like that of the tadpole, because God deeply cares for me.

To this the atheist will reply that if there is no God, the only things that matter are things that matter *to us*. What matters, they will say, is whether we live in such a way as to improve, however slightly, our lot and the lot of our fellow human beings. They will agree that without God there is no transcendent meaning or purpose of human life, but we just have to accept that point and do our best.

So again the deepest issue turns out to be whether God exists. If God exists, there *is* transcendent meaning to our lives. Whether we live or die, whether we thrive in life or flounder, whether we are moral or immoral, whether we love God or hate God—these things ultimately matter because they matter to our Creator.

## Human Suffering

The third point has to do with the fact that we live in a tough world. Many of us learned years ago, as first-year college students on the very first day in Economics 101, that the resources of life—food, shelter, a mother's love, good grades in school, a good job—are scarce, and so there will be competition for them. Sometimes the competition will be violent. Life is hard. We experience suffering, loss, pain and regret. Consequently I think another deep need of human beings is to avoid misfortune and suffering as much as possible for oneself and one's loved ones.

But we must be careful here: this does not mean that religious people fare better in this life than irreligious people. Despite those health-and-wealth or prosperity-gospel preachers we see on television, I have noticed no correlation whatsoever between being religious and suffering less, or between being irreligious and suffering more. Religion is not a rabbit's foot that keeps bad fortune away.

But if God exists, then quite apart from God's eschatological promises (which is a point I want to get to later), God offers us comfort, strength and guidance in the face of suffering. I once spoke to a religious skeptic who said he cringes whenever he hears religious people say, "I don't know how I could make it in life without God." He thought that was demeaning. But I don't react in that way at all to such talk. For believers in God, I think rejoicing in God's help in life is a perfectly valid thing to do. God promises to be with us in our suffering. We can have a kind of peace if we trust in God. Paul calls it "the peace of God, which surpasses all understanding" (Philippians 4:7).

We believe, as the great medieval mystic Julian of Norwich said, "And all shall be well, and all shall be well, and all manner of thing shall be well."[3] If God exists, you cannot only subjectively experience peace in the midst of trouble but actually experience peace that God gives you.

## The Problem of Guilt

The fourth point concerns the fact that we human beings like to think of ourselves as morally good. Despite that fact, I believe that almost all humans are troubled by guilt. We all know we have often failed to live up to our own or society's moral standards, let alone God's standards, if God exists. And some people are deeply troubled by feelings of guilt. Apart from God there are all kinds of secular ways of dealing with guilt—repressing it, punishing yourself, telling yourself that lots of people are worse than you, blaming your misdeeds on others (e.g., on the way your parents raised you) or getting therapy.

This raises a point that seems to bother nonbelievers. I have noticed that it troubles and insults them that Christians insist people are sinners. Many of them will say things like, "I know I'm not perfect; I make mistakes; I've done things I'm not proud of. But I think I'm a fairly moral person. So why are Christians so hung up on this 'Everybody is a sinner' kick?"

Since it clearly troubles people, let me say something about that point. When Christians say that all people are sinners, the

claim is not that all people are moral monsters like Hitler or
Stalin, or that they are as bad as they could possibly be. Christians
don't deny that some people are morally better than other people
or that people can perform morally good deeds.

Well, then what does it mean? It means that people fail to live
up to widely accepted moral standards, let alone God's standards.
Here's a thought experiment: Suppose we asked your grandmother
(or anybody you completely trust and would select) to follow you
around for two months or so and write down every moral or
ethical statement that you make. And suppose at the end of that
time we collate the statements—statements you've made like "It's
wrong to cheat on your income tax," "Don't lie to your parents" or
whatever—into a list of moral rules that we might call "Your
moral code" (or at least it would constitute much of it).

Next we ask your grandmother to follow you around for another
two months and record not your words but your deeds. The aim
is to find out whether you consistently follow the moral rules in
your own moral code. My point is this: if you're like me, you will
not succeed very well in following even your own moral precepts.
And that says nothing about the undoubtedly much stricter rules
that Christians say God has laid down in, say, the Ten
Commandments and the teachings of Jesus. Something close to
this is what I think Christians mean when they claim that we are
all sinners.[4]

So why does this amount to a problem that God can solve? It
is because if God exists, our guilt can be assuaged. God can make
our guilt objectively go away. He can forgive us. Of course the
atheist can then reply that this amounts to the idea that God
removes a problem—human guilt—that is only real if God exists.
But the answer is that our guilt is a problem without even
mentioning God. As I said, we don't even succeed in living up to

our own moral standards. And God can forgive the fact that we don't.

The atheist may well reply that the only people who are in a position to forgive a sin or fault are the people the sin was committed against. If some guy robs a colleague of mine of $100, I do not have the moral standing to forgive the thief, even if he repents and asks me to do so. Only my colleague can do that. This is true, but Christianity teaches that all sins are sins against God, as well as, of course, against the victim. All sins are violations of God's law. But the atheist has an answer to that: if God does not exist, there *are no* sins against God, and so of course God cannot grant forgiveness. But sins committed against other humans (lying to someone, stealing from someone) would still remain. Those sins can be forgiven only by the injured party.

No, they would not remain. On my view, if there were no God, there would be no sins of any kind because there would be no universe and thus no human beings. It is true that if—*per impossibile*—there is no God and everything else remains the same, then there are also no sins against God. But I still hold that there are no sins at all if God does not exist, because if God does not exist, nothing exists. Accordingly, what the atheist believes in—a world just like this one but *sans* God—is, in my opinion, impossible.

## Fear of Death

The fifth point has to do with fear of death and the deep human desire to survive, to live on after death. If God does not exist, and if (as atheists believe and as I deny as impossible) the world could still exist, there is very little hope of our surviving death. I happen to regard all attempts at what we might call "technological survival of death" as, well, slightly ridiculous. If my clone lives on, it will be genetically identical to me, but it won't be me; if my body is frozen at death, there is no good reason to think that people of the future will want to revive me even if they could; and a complete computer program of my brain state, even if implanted in an android that looks like me, will not in my opinion be me. But if an all-powerful God exists, God can ensure that we go on living after death.[5] In fact, in Christianity (and many other religions), God promises that that will happen.

But of course there is at least one after-life theory that on some versions of it are completely atheistic (like in some schools of Buddhism and Advaita Vedanta Hinduism). This theory is of course reincarnation. But I've never been convinced that the problem of personal identity in reincarnation can be solved, especially since neither the memory criterion nor the bodily criterion of personal identity is satisfied in putative cases of rebirth. Moreover, the very atheism of the theory (on its atheistic versions) presents a problem. How are karmic decisions made or karmic consequences arrived at apart from the existence of a personal God or karmic administrator? If there is a God or gods, or a person, or a committee of some sort, it is easy to imagine that being or beings saying to someone who has just died, "Okay, you were an evil merchant in Delhi in this previous life, but because of your bad karma I've now justly decided that you will be reborn as a beggar in Kolkata." That at least makes sense. But without any God or karmic administrator, I've never understood how such karmic "decisions" can be made. There can hardly be a natural law or set of natural laws that entail that a certain evil person will be reborn as a beggar in Kolkata as opposed to a leper in Mumbai. This picture is especially problematic since the idea in reincarnation is that such decisions are always entirely just and fair, never random or capricious.[6]

Moreover, an endless or almost endless cycle of life, death and rebirth, with all new incarnations based on karma from previous lives, is in my opinion not what most people who would prefer to live forever are looking for.

Let me return to a related point that I made in chapter one. It has to do with genocide and hope, although I realize that those two words do not often appear together in the same sentence. My argument is vaguely Kantian: unless God exists, our grounds for hope in the face of the Holocaust and other genocides are limited indeed. If no Creator or higher power such as the God of theism exists, the only hope that we can sensibly have, in my opinion, is tenuous and feeble. It would have to be the hope that some day we can design our educational, social, political and diplomatic systems in such a way that no more acts of genocide occur. I suppose in some sense we can *hope* for that outcome, but given human nature and the religious and ethnic hatreds that we see in the world it would be, again in my opinion, about like hoping that continental drift will cease.

As noted in chapter eight, if God does not exist, there is no hope whatsoever for any experience of reparation, justice or joy for the victims of genocide. They are dead and gone. That sort of hope makes sense only if God exists. If I were an atheist, and if my judgments about human nature led me to believe that murder and genocide can never be ruled out, well, that reasoning seems to me to lead to anguish and despair.

The atheist will reply that this life is all there is, that my death is the end of me and that I had best get on with the job of trying to live the best life that I can—which includes trying to do my small bit to prevent future murders and Holocausts. We live in a radically unjust world.

Still, I think most people have a deep longing for justice, and a hope that the world will turn out just. The reality of genocide in our world for me increases rather than decreases that hope. So

God can answer our longing for justice. I want to hope, as Julian said, that all will be well.

## Conclusion

So I cannot argue that religious people will all be happy and that religious skeptics will all be unhappy. And even if it is true, as I admit, that it is possible to be happy apart from God, that does not bother me. My argument instead is that part of the human predicament is that we have certain questions and desires that are not going to be answered if atheism is true. And they can be answered if God—or, more specifically the Christian God—exists.

# CONCLUSION

The Claremont Colleges, where I have taught for many years, is a consortium.[1] It is in Claremont, California, and it consists of five undergraduate colleges and two graduate institutions. The undergraduate colleges are highly selective and prestigious. All of them are completely secular and always have been.[2] Despite that fact, there has always existed a vibrant and active student Christian movement here under the influence of InterVarsity Christian Fellowship. Once, years ago, I signed a paper that indicated I was the faculty sponsor of InterVarsity on these campuses. For all I know, that may still be true. I am also occasionally asked to speak or serve on a panel at one of their meetings.

## Baptism

But my most memorable involvement with the Christian students here has to do with baptism. In May of every year, just after graduation, they have a week-long retreat at an InterVarsity-owned retreat center called Campus by the Sea. It is located on Santa Catalina, a lovely island some twenty-six miles west of Los Angeles in the Pacific Ocean. For about ten years the InterVarsity staff workers had me come to the island for one day of the week (usually a Thursday) because they wanted an ordained minister to conduct baptisms of students who had accepted Christ during the past school year. There were always other InterVarsity groups there that week as well, usually from the University of Southern California and the University of Nevada at Las Vegas.

Those baptisms were highlights of the school year for me. Here is what we did: We first gathered the whole camp (maybe 150 folks) in a room, where I briefly explained what Christian baptism is and why the church has always practiced it. I told them that baptism is a Christian sacrament for one reason and one reason only: Jesus commanded us to baptize. In what we call the Great Commission, he said, "Go therefore and make disciples of all nations, baptizing them in the name of the Father and of the Son and of the Holy Spirit" (Matthew 28:19). Then each student who was about to be baptized was asked to give a brief speech about his or her spiritual journey to that point. One year there were only three of them. Once I recall there were twelve. Usually the number was somewhere in-between. I explained that the reason we required this speech was because of what Paul said, "If you confess with your lips that Jesus is Lord and believe in your heart that God raised him from the dead, you will be saved" (Romans 10:9). The students had been prepared for baptism by one of the staff workers, usually Kate Vosburg, and they had clearly thought hard (and prayed!) about what they would say in front of their peers. After we heard from all of them, I had them answer four baptismal questions, and then we walked about two hundred yards down to the beach. There I called them one at a time into the ocean and baptized them in the name of the Father, the Son and the Holy Spirit. Then on the beach I had their friends and colleagues gather around each person, lay hands on them and offer prayers for their lifelong protection, their growth in the Holy Spirit and their service to the Lord. I then dismissed us with prayer and a benediction.

I want to focus on the speeches the students gave. They were told to explain to the rest of us why they had accepted Christ and wanted to be baptized. With great sincerity, they spoke of their spiritual struggles, the temptations that beset them, the love that Christian brothers and sisters had showed them, and their palpable relief at having finally decided to identify themselves with Christ and the Christian community. I cannot tell you how moving it was for me to listen to those talks.

Some of the obstacles they had faced were academic and intellectual in nature; they revolved around some of the same issues that we have discussed in this book. Others were more personal or even familial. One memorable student told us that she had been raised as an atheist and that her mother particularly hated Christianity. She said that her parents did not approve of her decision to become a Christian, and she envisioned difficulties ahead of her at home. She asked for our prayers. I remember admiring the courage of this young woman.[3]

I also want to stress that the students held that what they now believed was *true*. They were not saying anything like, "I really like Jesus, but of course somebody else might have another equally good savior." In submitting to baptism, they were not making a "lifestyle change"—they were bowing before the One they took to be *the truth* (John 14:6). I make this point because of the great influence of relativism in our culture today, especially on religious issues, as we discussed in chapter one. John Henry Newman, a nineteenth-century English Catholic whose works I admire, put it this way:

Liberalism in religion is the doctrine that there is no positive truth in religion, but that one creed is as good as another. . . . It is inconsistent with any recognition of any religion, as *true*. It teaches that all are to be tolerated, for all are matters of opinion. Revealed religion is not a truth, but a sentiment and a taste, not an objective fact, not miraculous; and it is the right of each individual to make it say just what strikes his fancy.[4]

I know that the students took their Christian beliefs to be objectively true because of the baptismal questions that they were required to answer.

*Question:* Do you believe in God the Father Almighty, Maker of heaven and earth: and in Jesus Christ His only Son our Lord: and in the Holy Spirit, the Lord and Giver of life?

*Answer:* I do.

*Question:* Do you confess your need of the forgiveness of sins and with a humble and contrite heart put your whole trust in the mercy of God, which is in Christ Jesus our Lord?

*Answer:* I do.

*Question:* Do you promise to make diligent use of the means of grace, to continue in the peace and fellowship of the people of God, and with the aid of the Holy Spirit to be Christ's faithful disciple to your life's end?[5]

*Answer:* I do.

*Question:* Do you desire to be baptized in this faith and to be received into membership in Christ's Church?

*Answer:* I do.[6]

The second question asks about putting your "whole trust in the mercy of God." I saw this trust clearly exemplified in 2008. This was near the beginning of the financial crisis that we now call the Great Recession. Late in the afternoon, after the baptisms, all the Claremont McKenna College seniors who were at the camp were gathered together for a photograph. There were ten or twelve of them; all had graduated the previous weekend. The US economy was bad, companies were not hiring, and I curiously asked the seniors about their immediate futures. The result was surprising. As I recall, only one had secured a good career-type job, one was heading for graduate school, and one or two others were looking hopefully at some employment possibilities. But the vast majority had nothing at all to report.

This was unusual. Ordinarily, well before graduation most of our seniors have jobs lined up and careers planned; those are the kinds of ambitious and competent students we have at our school. But as the unemployed alums spoke, I was heartened at the level of trust in God that they expressed. "I am concerned, but I am not going to be worried," one of them said, "God will provide." Another said, "There are not too many jobs out there at the moment; I may have to live at home for a while and volunteer somewhere or work at Starbucks, but I am confident that God will be with me."

## Conversion

Most of the students I baptized could be categorized as religious converts. Since it seems that most people most of the time stick with the religion (or irreligion) they were raised in, religious conversions are fairly unusual. But they do occur. A few of the students I baptized were raised in religious families. A few (like the student mentioned) were raised in decided irreligious families.

But I would say that most came from backgrounds that were at best only vaguely and nominally religious.

So what exactly is "religious conversion"? I will define it as a radical reorientation in religious outlook that has both cognitive aspects (there are new beliefs) and noncognitive aspects (there are new attitudes, values and behaviors). I suspect that conversions are usually the result of some sort of transformative experience, often involving a personal crisis. Some are sudden, all-at-once experiences, and others are more gradual. The converted person holds that her old beliefs and way of life were wrong or inadequate, and that a new direction in life is to be followed. The world is now seen differently than it was before. The convert is committed to a new worldview.

What then is Christian conversion? Well, obviously, it is conversion to Christianity. There are some paradigm cases known to most Christians (e.g., the conversion of the apostle Paul, recorded by Luke in Acts 9:1-19; see also Acts 22:6-16; 26:12-18; and the conversions of people like Augustine, John Wesley and C. S. Lewis). Conversion to Christianity must, as noted, involve both cognitive and noncognitive aspects. The cognitive aspects include certain core beliefs that the convert probably did not have before and now has (e.g., belief in the existence of the trinitarian God, or in one's own sinfulness, or in the incarnation and resurrection of Jesus). But, equally obviously, the cognitive aspect by itself is not enough. It is possible to believe the things that Christians believe but not be a Christian. There are things that we must not just believe but do (e.g., repent of our sins, worship God, try to live as Christ lived, help the poor, etc.). If converts do not do or sincerely attempt to do at least some of these things, they will not count as genuine converts to Christianity.

People notoriously disagree about the rationality of religious belief. Some argue that it is not rational; others claim that it is or at least can be rational. Naturally, I have no hope at all of settling that debate in this book. But I do want to ask an unusual question: Is the factor of religious conversion relevant to the debate? Does conversion contribute anything that might count toward rationality? I mean to understand *rationality* in a weak sense. The sentence "Jones is rational in believing p" just means that Jones is epistemologically entitled to believe p; in believing p, Jones cannot be considered gullible, credulous, insufficiently hardheaded, not sensible, thinking wishfully or the like. Rationality does not entail truth; it is possible rationally to believe something that is false. It is also possible for two people who disagree about the truth of some proposition both to be rational.[7]

My question then is this: Does or should the factor of religious conversion influence our views on the rationality of the convert's new beliefs? For example, suppose there are two people, Angelica and Blake, whose Christian beliefs and practices are quite similar. Suppose that Angelica was raised in a Christian family, never thought of herself as a non-Christian and never experienced a conversion experience. And suppose that Blake was not raised in a Christian family and had a conversion experience at a certain age. Again we assume that their religious beliefs and practices are roughly similar and also that their ability to defend their Christian beliefs and practices are roughly similar. My question then is, Other things being equal as much as possible, are Blake's Christian beliefs and orientation more rational than Angelica's because Blake is a convert?

Atheists, who usually hold that religious belief is not rational at all, will doubtless deny that conversion makes any difference. The fact that, say, the apostle Paul had a conversion experience makes his Christian beliefs no more rational than they would have been apart from any such experience. And atheists will quickly point out that lots of people are "converted" from religion to irreligion, which is certainly true.

However, it does seem that conversion stories do carry a certain psychological weight. Whether we agree with it or not, our interest is aroused when we hear a conversion story; we often listen carefully to the reasons the convert gives. "Once I was X and now, after a spiritual crisis, I am happily Y" amounts to the kind of story that people will usually listen to. Advocates of Y will often publicize or at least speak favorably about the narrative, as if it lends support to the truth or helpfulness of Y. And it does seem, as Nicholas Wolterstorff points out in a slightly different context, that in some cases God has to do something strange or uncanny to bring about a conversion, something that "stands out from the rumble of ordinary experience."[8] This certainly occurred in Paul's case.

There is no doubt that conversion experiences occur. The question is, What should we make of them? What is their best explanation? Do they or do they not add credence to the new position that the convert is now committed to? Christian converts will typically offer a narrative of their conversion experience that crucially involves the existence of God and the activity of God in their lives. The stories I heard on Catalina all did that. But it also seems possible to explain (or explain away) a typical religious conversion experience in an entirely naturalistic way. Indeed, this is often attempted. But of course the mere fact that such naturalistic explanations can be given does not mean that they amount to the true or best explanation. That remains to be decided.

I am going to argue that religious conversion experiences do or at least can lend a certain degree of credence to the truth or helpfulness of the religion converted to, and thus to the rationality of the converts in their new orientation. But first I want to explore one aspect of conversion experiences—namely, their privacy. I am thinking of the fact that conversion experiences are deeply convincing to the convert (of the truth of, say, Christianity) but not necessarily to anybody else. The convert takes his or her experience as an encounter with God, involving God's displeasure with his or her life, or God's grace, or God's guidance. But the point is that nobody else has that experience and so need not be convinced by it.

Accordingly, I will introduce a distinction between what I call public evidence and private evidence.[9] *Public evidence* in favor of a proposition p is evidence that in principle is available to all people and, if it is accepted as evidence in favor of p by one person, it ought to be accepted as evidence in favor of p by all people, or at least all rational people. Suppose my evidence for the claim that Julius Caesar was the first Roman emperor is that I read a statement to that effect in a world-history textbook. There may be people who would not consider that evidence to be conclusive (mistakes do occasionally work their way into history textbooks), but even those folks ought to accept that the evidence cited at least counts in favor of the claim. Accordingly, it is public evidence.

*Private evidence* in favor of p, on the other hand, is evidence for p that is available to only one person (or perhaps a group of persons) and need not be accepted as evidence in favor of p by any other person (or by persons outside the group). There are two conditions here: if the evidence is private to me, (1) only I have direct access to it, and (2) I am the only one who finds it convincing or even as counting as evidence. The fact that I had a conversion experience that convinces me that God exists may constitute evidence for me that God exists, but it need not be accepted as evidence in favor of God's existence by anybody else. Private evidence is evidence only to the person who had the private experience.

The distinction between the two sorts of evidence is not rigorous; it certainly raises questions that I do not want to address here. For example, what is meant by "access"? Can't other people have access to my private evidence in the sense of clearly understanding it, even if it just amounts to their hearing or reading an account of my conversion experience? Moreover, it seems at least possible that someone else might find my private evidence convincing. "Well, if you believe in God because of your conversion experience, that is enough for me," so this person might say. Still, even at this imprecise and slippery level, I think the distinction between the two sorts of evidence can be helpful.

Now my argument is that a convert is rational in his or her new orientation (based on private evidence) only if certain criteria are satisfied. But first I want to point out that virtually everybody relies on private evidence in determining his or her opinions. Let's begin with philosophers: concerning certain metaphysical, epistemological and ethical problems, they notoriously hold strong beliefs that cannot be proved and that are highly controversial in philosophical circles. Indeed, philosophers write articles and books defending those positions. Their evidence is not accepted by other philosophers. This would include beliefs, for example, about whether determinism is compatible with moral responsibility, whether humans have immaterial minds, whether the correspondence theory of truth is defensible or whether everyone has a right to a living wage. There are even beliefs that virtually every philosopher (and nonphilosopher) holds that cannot be proved in a non-question-begging way (e.g., that our senses are normally reliable, that other people have minds or even that the external world exists).

Doubtless there are areas of life where the standards of evidence are rigorous and need to be so. In the court room, for example, in criminal cases, American juries are asked to convict a defendant only if there is "no reasonable doubt" that the defendant is guilty. Similarly, in most scientific endeavors, the standards of evidence and of rational belief are and ought to be high. Private evidence will rarely be allowable there.

Still, in the moral and political realms, not only philosophers but virtually all people have beliefs that are confidently and even passionately held, beliefs that cannot be proved and that are equally strongly opposed by other people. Is capital punishment ever morally justified? Should the United States have universal health care? Do animals have rights? We simply cannot show that our beliefs on these and other such points are based on conclusive public evidence—indeed, the evidence that convinces us is often not accepted by others—but we still hold them.[10]

As noted, I wish to argue that a conversion experience can add to our assessment of the rationality of the new orientation of the convert. But the point holds only if certain criteria are met. I will now discuss four such conditions.

1. *The propositions that the convert now believes cannot be falsified by public evidence; neither the story itself nor the religion that the convert is converted to are subject to defeaters.* If the convert's narrative contains serious inconsistencies, we will clearly be inclined to dismiss it. If the position or religion that the person has been converted to contains tenets that are known to be false or subject to powerful defeaters, we will judge that he or she is not being rational. This criterion importantly answers an objection that someone might raise—that I have opened the door too widely to irrational beliefs. Can't people claim that they have had a "conversion experience" based on private evidence to astrology or to the view that the earth is flat or to a religion that says that aliens occasionally visit the earth and must be worshiped? Of course not. Those views are, in my opinion, subject to overwhelming defeaters.

2. *The convert is, so far as we can tell, sincere and honest in telling his or her story.* We can imagine, and have perhaps encountered, conversion narratives that are self-serving or insincere. In such cases, we will be inclined to dismiss the story and hold that the convert is not being rational. Sincerity, as I understand it, includes the notion that the private evidence that the convert experienced in the conversion experience is indeed deeply convincing to him or her. This condition is satisfied if the convert makes a convincing case that he or she is being truthful.

3. *So far as we can tell, in the conversion experience the convert had no rational choice but to decide between the old way of life and the new way of life.* I am thinking here of cases where, because of the circumstances and pressures of life, the potential convert feels strongly that he or she must make a decision between the old and the new way of life. I once knew a college student who was torn and very much in crisis. He telephoned me at home one evening and said he had to talk to me as soon as possible. The problem was that he was a hard-charging, high-achieving young man who longed for "success"; he wanted to graduate, go out into the world and make millions of dollars. But he also felt a strong attraction toward a certain religious sect that he had been meeting with and that demanded almost total commitment to its programs. He had to decide what to do. In such cases, suspension of judgment between the two alternatives is not pragmatically possible. If the other criteria are also satisfied, it is rational for the person to convert.

4. *The conversion results in superior values and increased moral behavior on the part of the convert.* Although it would not prove the rationality of a new religious orientation, this is an important criterion from a Christian point of view. Christians will be suspicious of any conversion experience that does not lead to Christian values and Christian behavior.

When these four conditions are met—so I am claiming—the convert is rational in holding to the new position. This certainly does seem to apply to the conversion of Paul. First, he was converted to a religion that crucially entails certain claims that have not been disproved or subjected to compelling defeaters (e.g., God exists; Jesus is Lord; justification is by faith). The falsity or improbability of these claims is not provable by public evidence. Second, Paul's own account of his conversion (Galatians 1:13–2:14) certainly seems sincere and in the main consistent with Luke's accounts of Paul's conversion in Acts. Third, the accounts in Acts of Paul's conversion experience on the road to Damascus certainly present a case where Paul was justified in converting because he had no real option to suspend judgment on whether to convert or not. Fourth, Paul's conversion does seem to have produced enhanced ethical behavior. After his conversion, he does not strike us as a perfect human being, but there was no more behavior of the preconversion sort that Luke describes as "still breathing out threats and murder against the disciples of the Lord" (Acts 9:1; cf. Acts 8:1).

But what about my claim that conversion adds to the case for rationality?[11] My argument to that effect has primarily to do with criteria 2 and 3. Criterion 1 is external to the convert's conversion narrative and is not directly related to how convincing it is; and criterion 4 has to do with the ethical results of the conversion. But the second and third criteria are both crucially related to the question of how believable and convincing the conversion narrative is. Religious conversion, in the case of these criteria, adds something. If the narrative is believable, it adds something that would not have been there had there been no conversion. Converts can give reasons for their conversion.

It is clear that I found the speeches by the students on Catalina Island to be deeply impressive and convincing. Doubtless the primary reason is that I was already a member of the faith they were joining. I was ready to accept what they said. Still, I think their accounts of their conversion to Christ satisfy the criteria I've just enumerated.

## Rationality

In closing, I would like to emphasize the limited nature of my argument in this chapter. I have not argued that all Christian claims are true. I have not even argued that it is irrational not to believe them. But it is clear that no criticism of religion and religious people is more common these days than the claim that it is irrational to be religious. Here is an example. (I could have chosen from among many other such statements from contemporary religious skeptics). Atheist philosopher Kai Nielsen declares, "Religious belief—or at least belief in God—should be impossible for someone living in our century, who thinks carefully about these matters and who has a tolerable scientific education and good philosophical training."[12]

In the light of the argument just given, this sort of criticism of religious or Christian belief collapses. Religious belief can be rational, and religious conversion can help establish its rationality.

There is no doubt that being a Christian in secular academia these days is difficult, for both students and faculty. But during my career I have been immeasurably encouraged and strengthened by the Christian students and colleagues I have met in Claremont and elsewhere, both those students I was privileged to baptize and many others. I hope this book can also be a help to those who read it.

# FURTHER READING

The following are some books that can be helpful to Christian students at secular colleges and universities, as well as other folks.

Beckwith, Francis J., William Lane Craig, and J. P. Moreland, eds. *To Everyone An Answer: A Case for the Christian Worldview*. Downers Grove, IL: InterVarsity Press, 2004.

Butterfield, Rosaria Champagne. *The Secret Thoughts of an Unlikely Convert: An English Professor's Journey into Christian Faith*. Pittsburgh: Crown & Covenant, 2012.

Craig, William Lane. *Reasonable Faith: Christian Truth and Apologetics*. 3rd ed. Wheaton, IL: Crossway Books, 2008.

Davis, Stephen T. *Christian Philosophical Theology*. Oxford: Oxford University Press, 2016.

Evans, C. Stephen. *Why Christian Faith Still Makes Sense: A Response to Contemporary Challenges*. Grand Rapids: Baker Academic, 2015.

Habermas, Gary, and Michael Licona. *The Case for the Resurrection*. Grand Rapids: Kregel, 2004.

Kreeft, Peter, and Ronald K. Tacelli. *Handbook of Christian Apologetics: Hundreds of Answers to Crucial Questions*. Downers Grove, IL: InterVarsity Press, 1994.

Metaxas, Eric. *Socrates in the City: Conversations on "Life, God, and Other Small Topics."* New York: Dutton, 2011.

Murray, Michael J. *Reason for the Hope Within*. Grand Rapids: Eerdmans, 1999.

Poplin, Mary. *Is Reality Secular? Testing the Assumptions of Four Global Worldviews*. Downers Grove, IL: InterVarsity Press, 2014.

Swinburne, Richard. *Is There a God?* Oxford: Oxford University Press, 2010.

# NOTES

### Chapter 1: Is There Any Such Thing as Objective Truth?

[1]This chapter appears here for the first time. Its ancestor is a lecture delivered to a faculty retreat at Azusa Pacific University in August 2011.

[2]Thomas Aquinas, *Summa Theologica* 1.16.21 (New York: Benziger, 1947), 90. In this translation, the statement says, "Truth is defined by conformity of intellect and thing."

[3]Max Horkheimer, "Theism and Atheism," *Critique of Instrumental Reason* (New York: Continuum, 1974), 47.

[4]Kai Nielsen, "Why Should I Be Moral?," *American Philosophical Quarterly* 21, no. 1 (January 1984): 91.

[5]Richard Taylor, *Ethics, Faith, and Reason* (Englewood Cliffs, NJ: Prentice Hall, 1985), 7.

[6]See William Lane Craig, "The Indispensability of Theological Meta-Ethical Foundations for Morality," www.leaderu.com/offices/billcraig /docs/meta-eth.html. The quotations in the previous two footnotes are cited in Craig.

[7]I borrow this argument, with some modifications, from Professor Douglas Geivett of Biola University. I use it with his permission.

### Chapter 2: Why Believe in God?

[1]Richard Dawkins, *The God Delusion* (New York: Houghton Mifflin, 2006).

[2]"Theistic proof" is a term that philosophers use for an argument in favor of the existence of God.

[3]For a more complete version of the argument, see chapter two of Stephen T. Davis, *Christian Philosophical Theology* (Oxford: Oxford University Press, 2006).

[4]I will understand a NB to be a being that (1) is everlasting and (2) depends for its existence on no other being. In some strong sense of the word *cannot*, a NB cannot not exist. A contingent being, on the other hand, is a being that can either exist or not exist. If it exists, it depends, while it exists, on another being or beings for its existence. Although I think it is logically possible for there to be an everlasting contingent being (if God, for example, keeps it in existence at all times), apart from that (in my opinion, unactualized) possibility, contingent beings have finite lifespans.

[5]A slightly weaker version of the PSR says this: Everything that comes into existence has a reason for its existence. I opt for the stronger version so that the PSR will apply to the universe even if it turns out that the universe is everlasting (if there is no moment of time when it does not exist) and thus did not come into existence. This is because even if the universe is eternal, the question "Why should it exist instead of not exist?" is still a legitimate question. One problem with the stronger version of the PSR is that it requires that even NBs (if there are any) have a reason for their existence. But then we can say that the reason for the existence of a given NB is simply that it is a NB.

[6]Richard Taylor, *Metaphysics*, 4th ed. (Englewood Cliffs, NJ: Prentice Hall, 1992), 101.

[7]As indeed I argued in Stephen T. Davis, *God, Reason, and Theistic Proofs* (Edinburgh: Edinburgh University Press, 1997), 144-46. The present chapter represents a correction of the argument presented there. John Hick has also argued that the CA begs the question. See John Hick, ed., *The Existence of God* (New York: Macmillan, 1964), 6-7.

[8]For discussion of them, see Davis, *God, Reason, and Theistic Proofs*, 70-76.

[9]Frederick Copleston, quoted in Hick, *Existence of God*, 174-77.

[10]Bertrand Russell, quoted in ibid., 175, 177.

[11]Copleston, reprinted in ibid., 93.

[12]This argument is discussed by Alvin Plantinga in *The Nature of Necessity* (Oxford: Clarendon Press, 1974), 217-18.

[13]It should be noted that attempts have been made to argue against the PSR, but they are not convincing. (1) Some have argued that since quantum physics, at least on some interpretations, allows for undetermined and inexplicable *events*, it can also allow for *things* to come into existence

uncaused. But even if indeterministic interpretations of certain quantum events are correct, the conservation laws in physics still rule out things coming into existence uncaused. (2) Others argue that the uncaused and totally random coming into existence of something is not logically contradictory, and indeed is perfectly conceivable. Both points are true, but prove nothing. There are lots of reasons why a given proposition might be intellectually unacceptable besides its being logically contradictory. And in some sense of the word *conceive*, I can surely conceive of, say, a poodle popping into existence in my office for no cause or reason. But that does nothing to show that belief that such an event can occur is plausible.

[14] See J. L. Mackie, *The Miracle of Theism* (Oxford: Oxford University Press, 1982), 82-87.

[15] Taylor, *Metaphysics*, 101.

[16] As William L. Craig argues. See his "Scientific Confirmation of the Cosmological Argument," in Louis P. Pojman, *Philosophy of Religion*, 4th ed. (Belmont, CA: Wadsworth, 2002), 32.

[17] There is a problem with the atheist's theory that I will note but not explore. It was originally pointed out by A. N. Prior that it cannot be the case that only certain things and not others come into existence uncaused because, before they exist, there is simply nothing that would determine that only things of that kind can come into existence uncaused. Why then is it that animals, automobiles and houses cannot come into existence uncaused, but the universe can? See A. N. Prior, "Limited Indeterminism," in *Papers on Time and Tense* (Oxford: Clarendon Press, 1968), 65.

[18] J. P. Moreland and Kai Nielsen, eds., *Does God Exist? The Great Debate* (Nashville: Thomas Nelson, 1990), 48.

[19] Augustine, *Confessions* 1.1.

## Chapter 3: Is the Bible's Picture of Jesus Reliable?

[1] The present chapter is largely based on Stephen T. Davis, "The Gospels Are Reliable as Historically Factual Accounts," in *Debating Christian Theism*, ed. J. P. Moreland, Chad Meister and Khaldoun A. Sweis (Oxford: Oxford University Press, 2013).

[2] Besides the discrepancies, the central reason that I do not affirm inerrancy is that commitment to it drives interpreters toward forced and awkward interpretations of the Bible in order to make problematic assertions be true.

[3]But I discuss this point in chapter one of Stephen T. Davis, *Making Sense of the Resurrection* (Grand Rapids: Eerdmans, 1993). See also Stephen T. Davis, *God, Reason, and Theistic Proofs* (Edinburgh: Edinburgh University Press, 1997).

[4]I am indebted to Craig Blomberg for this example.

[5]Richard Bauckham, *Jesus and the Eyewitnesses* (Grand Rapids: Eerdmans, 2006), 6, 8, 93, 503.

[6]See, for example, Bart Ehrman, *Jesus, Interrupted* (New York: HarperCollins, 2009), 181-224.

[7]Indeed, one sometimes gets the impression that in such circles any and all hypotheses about Jesus, however remote and bizarre they might be, are acceptable topics of serious scholarly discussion—except, of course, orthodox ones.

[8]A typical list is found in Norman Perrin, *The New Testament: An Introduction* (New York: Harcourt, Brace, Jovanovich, 1974), 287-88.

[9]Marcus Borg insisted that these last items all arose vis-à-vis the post-Easter Jesus. And he was certainly right that it was in the post-Easter period that these notions were spelled out. But my question is, What was it about the disciples' experience of the pre-Easter Jesus that made it possible for them later to arrive at such lofty notions?

[10]Charles Moule, "Three Points of Conflict in the Christological Debate," in *Incarnation and Myth: The Debate Continued*, ed. Michael Goulder (Grand Rapids: Eerdmans, 1979), 137; see also Moule's *The Origin of Christology* (Cambridge: Cambridge University Press, 1977), 2-7; Martin Hengel, *The Son of God* (Philadelphia: Fortress, 1976), 2, 10; see also Hengel's *Between Jesus and Paul* (Philadelphia: Fortress, 1983), 31; Wright's views on this point are summarized in Marcus Borg and N. T. Wright, *The Meaning of Jesus* (New York: HarperCollins, 2007), 157-68; Larry W. Hurtado, "Pre-70 C. E. Jewish Opposition to Christ-Devotion," *Journal of Theological Studies* 50, no. 1 (April 1999): 5-6, 10.

[11]Arthur Wainwright argues convincingly that on several crucial Christological points, the New Testament writers agree. See his *Beyond Biblical Criticism: Encountering Jesus in Scripture* (Atlanta: John Knox, 1982), 22-33.

[12]These points are explored more fully in chapter five of Stephen T. Davis, *Christian Philosophical Theology* (Oxford: Oxford University Press, 2006).

[13]Obviously, I do not claim that the canonical Gospels or even Mark are simply reproduced in Paul or vice versa. Indeed, some of the items just

mentioned are not in Mark at all (e.g., resurrection appearances only occur in Mark's inauthentic long ending), and many items from the Gospels (notably miracle stories and parables) are not mentioned in the Pauline letters. But the basic outline is there.

[14]I explore this issue in more detail in chapter nine of *Christian Philosophical Theology*.

[15]See Stephen T. Davis, "'Who Can Forgive Sins But God Alone?': Jesus, Forgiveness, and Divinity," in *The Multivalence of Biblical Texts and Theological Meanings*, ed. Christine Helmer (Atlanta: Society of Biblical Literature, 2006), 113-23.

[16]I do not claim that Jesus went around saying "I am God" or thought of himself in the creedal terms arrived at centuries later—terms like "hypostatic union," "Second Person of the Trinity," etc.

[17]I have argued elsewhere (following Royce Gruenler) that a plausible case can be made for Jesus' messianic consciousness even from sayings in the Gospels that New Testament critics accept as authentic. See Stephen T. Davis, "Was Jesus Mad, Bad, or God?" in *The Incarnation*, ed. Stephen T. Davis, Daniel Kendall and Gerald O'Collins (Oxford: Oxford University Press, 2002), 234-39.

[18]This point will be considered in more detail in chapter four.

[19]Among many others, see Richard Swinburne, *The Resurrection of God Incarnate* (Oxford: Oxford University Press, 2003); and N. T. Wright, *The Resurrection of the Son of God* (Minneapolis: Fortress Press, 2003).

[20]I think especially here of the work of Richard Swinburne. See, for example, *The Existence of God* (Oxford: Oxford University Press, 1979).

[21]Again, see chapter four. See also Stephen T. Davis, *Risen Indeed* (Grand Rapids: Eerdmans, 1993).

[22]William Lane Craig makes this point convincingly. See chapter eight of his *Reasonable Faith*, 3rd ed. (Wheaton, IL: Crossway, 2008).

[23]The rule of faith was the church fathers' term for the church's view of the overall message of Scripture.

[24]Several of these points were suggested years ago by E. J. Carnell in his *The Case for Orthodox Theology* (Philadelphia: Westminster Press, 1959), 51-65.

[25]See Stephen T. Davis, *The Debate About the Bible: Inerrancy Verses Infallibility* (Louisville, KY: Westminster Press, 1977).

[26]I would like to thank Professors Craig Evans and Alex Rajczi for their helpful comments.

## Chapter 4: Was Jesus Raised from the Dead?

[1]I have, however, argued this point in much more detail on other occasions. See, for example, Stephen T. Davis, *Risen Indeed: Making Sense of the Resurrection* (Grand Rapids: Eerdmans, 1993); and chapter five of Stephen T. Davis, *Disputed Issues: Contending for Christian Faith in Today's Academic Setting* (Waco, TX: Baylor University Press, 2009).

[2]Josephus, *Antiquities of the Jews* 4.8.15.

[3]Richard Swinburne, *The Resurrection of God Incarnate* (Oxford: Oxford University Press, 2003).

[4]See, for example, ibid., 174-86.

## Chapter 5: Does Evolution Disprove Christianity?

[1]Charles Darwin, *The Origin of Species by Means of Natural Selection* (London: Murray, 1859).

[2]Richard Dawkins, *The Blind Watchmaker* (New York: W. W. Norton, 1986), 10.

[3]His dating system was based on the biblical genealogies (e.g., Genesis 5; Matthew 1:1-16; Luke 3:23-38).

[4]There are many other powerful reasons to hold that the earth is ancient. See Denis Alexander, *Creation or Evolution: Do We Have to Choose?* (Oxford: Monarch Books, 2008).

[5]ID is not strictly speaking an alternative to the two creationist views just discussed. Some defenders of ID identify themselves as old earth creationists. ID is best understood as a methodological position that can be compatible with either of the creationist theories or even, in my opinion, with theistic evolution. But it deserves separate treatment.

[6]I do not have the space to discuss the many instances of fine-tuning that are mentioned, but a brief discussion of several of them can be found in Stephen T. Davis, *God, Reason, and Theistic Proofs* (Edinburgh: Edinburgh University Press, 1997), 107-11.

[7]Ross lists twenty-five aspects of cosmic fine-tuning. See Hugh Ross, "Astronomical Evidence for a Personal, Transcendent God," in *The Creation Hypothesis: Scientific Evidence for an Intelligent Designer*, ed. J. P. Moreland (Downers Grove, IL: InterVarsity Press, 1994), 160-63.

[8]Michael J. Behe, *Darwin's Black Box* (New York: Free Press, 1996).

[9]See William A. Dembski, *Intelligent Design* (Downers Grove, IL: InterVarsity Press, 1999).

¹⁰See, for example, Stephen C. Meyer, *Darwin's Doubt: The Explosive Origin of Animal Life and the Case for Intelligent Design* (New York: HarperOne, 2013), 389-91.

¹¹Kenneth R. Miller, *Only a Theory: Evolution and the Battle for America's Soul* (New York: Penguin, 2008), 101-8.

¹²Kenneth R. Miller, "Answering the Biochemical Argument from Design," in *God and Design: The Teleological Argument and Modern Science*, ed. Neil Manson (London: Routledge, 2003), 302-5. See also Alexander, *Creation or Evolution*, 297-304; and Miller, *Only a Theory*, 53-87.

¹³Michael Ruse, "Modern Biologists and the Argument from Design," in Manson, *God and Design*, 316-17.

¹⁴Metaphysical naturalism is roughly the view that says (1) the physical universe (atoms in motion) is all that there is; there are no nonphysical things like God, gods, angels, spirits or souls; and (2) there are no nonnatural events; everything that occurs can in principle be explained by methods similar to those that are used in the natural sciences. There are no miracles, interventions in the natural order or in-principle inexplicable events.

¹⁵David Atkinson, *The Message of Genesis 1–11* (Downers Grove, IL: InterVarsity Press, 1990), 31.

¹⁶The word *theory* has many meanings. Here it refers to a well-established but unproven body of scientific claims that attempt to explain certain known facts.

¹⁷As we see preeminently (but not only) in the Burgess shelf in Canada, where very many fossils of strange and exotic animals from the mid-Cambrian Period are preserved.

¹⁸See Alexander, *Creation or Evolution*, 126-29.

¹⁹Kelly James Clark, *Religion and the Sciences of Origins: Historical and Contemporary Discussions* (New York: Palgrave Macmillan, 2014), 89-90. See also pp. 90–96 for other evidences for evolution that I have not mentioned.

²⁰DNA is the molecule in cells that contains coded information that directs the development of all living things. See Stephen Freeland, "The Evolutionary Origin of Genetic Information," *Perspectives on Science and Christian Faith* 63, no. 4 (December 2011): 241-42.

²¹Ibid., 245, 250.

²²Alexander, *Creation or Evolution*, 119.

²³See Clark, *Religion and the Sciences of Origins*, 102.

24With the recent upswing in astronomical searches for earth-like planets in our galaxy, the possibility that life on earth originated elsewhere in the galaxy or universe is now being taken seriously in some circles. I am not going to discuss the point here, however, because that research does not address the question of the absolute origin of life.

25See, for example, Phillip E. Johnson, *Darwin on Trial* (Downers Grove, IL: InterVarsity Press, 1993), 27, 50-51.

26See Niles Eldredge and Stephen Jay Gould, "Punctuated Equilibria: An Alternative to Phyletic Gradualism," *Evolution*, accessed April 7, 2016, http://blackwellpublishing.com/ridley/classictexts/eldredge.asp.

27C. John Collins, *Genesis 1–4: A Linguistic, Literary, and Theological Commentary* (Phillipsburg, NJ: Presbyterian & Reformed, 2003), quoted in Tim Keller, "Creation, Evolution, and Christian Laypeople," *BioLogos*, March 2012, http://biologos.org/blogs/archive/series/ creation-evolution-and-christian-laypeople. Keller's essay has been helpful to me at several points.

28I would like to thank Professors David Vosburg and Alan Padgett for their helpful comments on an earlier draft of this chapter.

## Chapter 6: Can Cognitive Science Explain Religion?

1This essay appears here for the first time, although a few parts of it (see endnote 26) have been published earlier.

2See, for example, Pascal Boyer, *The Naturalness of Religious Ideas: A Cognitive Theory of Religion* (Berkeley: University of California Press, 1994).

3For example, Paul Bloom claims that religious belief is "an incidental by-product of cognitive functioning gone awry" (Paul Bloom, "Is God an Accident?" *Atlantic Monthly* [December 2005]: 105-12).

4A spandrel is a characteristic of an organism that is an evolutionary byproduct—that is, not directly due to adaptive selection.

5Notice that I am not using the word *natural* here to mean "adaptive," as it is sometimes used in CSR circles. Nor am I considering senses like "inborn" or the opposite of "artificial."

6Obviously, religions involve much more than just beliefs—there are rituals, ethical commands, holidays, buildings, and customs about food, clothing, marriage and the like—and that point will turn out to be important later.

7I do not intend to discuss the suggested mechanisms in any detail in the present chapter, because CSR scholars disagree over what they are. Several quite different explanations of religion have been suggested, and not all of them are consistent with each other. Is religion maladaptive or adaptive (or perhaps a spandrel of other adaptive behaviors)? Is religion to be explained primarily in evolutionary or cognitive terms? And what are the most important evolutionary or cognitive mechanisms that produce religion?

[8]Of course there are nonbelievers who will concede that some religious believers may be rational in believing (e.g., in God, given what they know or rationally believe).

[9]In the present chapter, I will focus mainly on Christianity. This is the religion I know best and am most confident about so far as my overall argument is concerned. But I want to be clear that my argument is meant to hold for other religions too—namely, those that are also highly costly in an evolutionary or even nonevolutionary sense. References to God can be taken to refer to "God, gods, or other supernatural beings."

[10]Much of this and the next section is based on chapter one of Stephen T. Davis, *Christian Philosophical Theology* (Oxford: Oxford University Press, 2006).

[11]Interestingly, hardness of heart in the mind of a person is sometimes said to be the work of God (Exodus 4:21; 7:3; 14:4, 17; Deuteronomy 2:30; Joshua 11:20; Isaiah 63:17; Romans 9:18) and sometimes the work of the person whose heart is hardened (Exodus 8:32; 9:34-35; Deuteronomy 15:7; 2 Chronicles 36:13; Psalm 95:8; Hebrews 3:13; 4:7). I will not ask whether God's hardening of peoples' hearts and people hardening their own hearts refer to separate occasions of hardening or whether it makes sense to consider that the same event of hardening can be caused both by God and the person.

[12]Perhaps it is related to the dual processing that Tamar Gendler writes about. See her "Alief and Beliefs," *Journal of Philosophy* 105, no. 10 (October 2008).

[13]V. Reynolds and R. Tanner, *The Social Ecology of Religion* (New York: Oxford University Press, 1995).

[14]Richard Sosis and Candace Alcorta, "Signaling, Solidarity, and the Sacred: The Evolution of Religious Behavior," *Evolutionary Anthropology* 12 (2003). But see Michael J. Murray and Lyn Moore, "Costly Signaling and the Origin of Religion," *Journal of Cognition and Culture* 9 (2009).

[15]There are of course costs involved in *not* being religious in parts of the world.

[16]Perhaps these points amount to some of the reasons why Thomas Nagel, an intellectually honest man, admits that he does not *want* God to exist. He says, "I want atheism to be true and am made uneasy by the fact that some of the most intelligent and well-informed people I know are religious believers. It isn't just that I don't believe in God and, naturally, hope that I'm right in my belief. It's that I hope there is no God! I don't want there to be a God; I don't want the universe to be like that" (Thomas Nagel, *The Last Word* [New York: Oxford University Press, 1997], 130).

[17]See Alvin Plantinga, "Games Scientists Play," in *The Believing Primate*, ed. Jeffrey Schloss and Michael Murray (Oxford: Oxford University Press, 2009), 144. See also Alvin Plantinga, *Where the Conflict Really Lies: Science, Religion, and Naturalism* (Oxford: Oxford University Press, 2011), 146-47.

[18]The issue is more complicated than this; nevertheless, I stand by my "surely not" comment. I explore the matter in some detail in Stephen T. Davis, "Pascal on Self-Caused Belief" in *Religious Studies* 27, no. 1 (March 1991): 27-37. See also Stephen T. Davis, *God, Reason, and Theistic Proofs* (Edinburgh: Edinburgh University Press, 1997), 160-62.

[19]These and other objections are explained and carefully answered in Michael Murray, "Scientific Explanations of Religion and the Justification of Religious Belief," in *Believing Primate*, 168-78.

[20]Matthew Alper, *The God Part of the Brain* (New York: Rogue Press, 2000), 79.

[21]The one missing piece in the attempt to explain the existence of the phenomenon of religion along cognitive and evolutionary lines, in my opinion, is what Calvin called the *sensus divinitatus*. This is the sense of God, the capacity to know God and the need for fellowship with God that (so Christians believe) God implants in human beings. Add that into the mix, and we may then have an adequate explanation.

[22]Many others besides me have made this point. See, for example, Michael Murray, "Evolutionary Explanations of Religion," in *God Is Great, God Is Good*, ed. William Lane Craig and Chad Meister (Downers Grove, IL: InterVarsity Press, 2009), 91-106.

[23]As is clearly pointed out in Kelly James Clark and Justin L. Barrett, "Reidian Religious Epistemology and the Cognitive Science of Religion," *Journal of the American Academy of Religion* 79, no. 3 (September 2011): 660. Barrett is one of the foremost Christian scholars in this field and has influenced much of my thinking in this chapter.

²⁴Murray makes some of these same points. See his *Believing Primate*, 176.

²⁵Augustine, *The Confessions of St. Augustine* (London: Thomas Nelson, n.d.), 1.

²⁶I would like to thank Michael Murray, Colin Ruloff, Michael Spezio and the members of the Claremont Colleges philosophy "work in progress" group (especially Michael Green, Amy Kind, Alex Rajczi and Peter Ross) for their helpful comments on an earlier draft of this chapter. I would also like to thank the members of the philosophy department at California State University at San Bernardino (especially Jill Buroker, Matthew Davidson and Tony Roy) for the helpful comments.

## Chapter 7: Is Christianity Unique?

¹This chapter was originally a Veritas Forum talk delivered at Pomona College on October 9, 2008.

²In some ways this threefold dichotomy can be misleading, but it will do for our purposes. See Harold Netland, "Religious Exclusivism," in *Philosophy of Religion: Classical and Contemporary Issues*, ed. Paul Copan and Chad Meister (Malden, MA: Blackwell, 2008).

³See Karl Rahner, "Anonymous Christians," "Anonymous Christianity and the Missionary Task of the Church," and "The One Christ and the Universality of Salvation," all reprinted in Karl Rahner, *Theological Investigations* (New York: Crossroads), vols. 6, 12 and 16, respectively.

⁴The term *pluralism* is used variously. Sometimes it means the simple fact that there are various religions in the world. Sometimes it means having a courteous and open-minded attitude toward people of other religions than one's own. These definitions do not necessarily imply relativism.

⁵John Hick, *An Interpretation of Religion* (London: Macmillan, 1989).

⁶See John Hick, *The Metaphor of God Incarnate: Christology in a Pluralistic Age* (Louisville, KY: Westminster John Knox Press, 1993).

⁷Timothy O'Connor, "Religious Pluralism," in *Reason for the Hope Within*, ed. Michael J. Murray (Grand Rapids: Eerdmans, 1999), 174-75.

⁸See Stephen T. Davis, *Risen Indeed* (Grand Rapids: Eerdmans, 1993), chap. 8.

⁹This is not to deny the importance of Christian involvement in social and moral issues. After all, Jesus not only preached to people about God and counseled spiritually confused people; he also fed the hungry, healed the sick and worked to overturn unjust social and economic practices. We cut

the gospel in half if we do evangelism without social action or social action without evangelism.

[10]Robert W. Wood, ed., "Tillich Encounters Japan," *Japanese Religions*, May 1961, 2:48-71. See also Harold Netland, *Encountering Religious Pluralism* (Downers Grove, IL: InterVarsity Press, 2001), 339.

[11]See more detailed arguments in Stephen T. Davis, *Risen Indeed: Making Sense of the Resurrection* (Grand Rapids: Eerdmans, 1993).

[12]See part two of Stephen T. Davis, *Christian Philosophical Theology* (Oxford: Oxford University Press, 2006).

## Chapter 8: Do Evil and Suffering Show
## That God Does Not Exist?

[1]Alvin Plantinga, *God, Freedom, and Evil* (New York: Harper & Row, 1974), 27-28.

[2]For my more complete thoughts on this subject, see Stephen T. Davis, *Encountering Evil: Live Options in Theodicy*, 2nd ed. (Louisville, KY: Westminster John Knox Press, 2001); and "Horrendous Evils and Christ," in *The History of Evil*, ed. Jerome Gellman (New York: Routledge, forthcoming).

[3]I do not wish to be interpreted as denying the possibility that members of other religions can also solve the problem of evil via their own theological commitments.

[4]She defines *horrors* as "evil the participation in which (that is, the doing or suffering of which) constitutes prima facie reasons to doubt whether the participant's life could (given their inclusion in it) be a great good to him/her on the whole" (Marilyn Adams, *Horrendous Evils and the Goodness of God* [New York: Cornell University Press, 1999], 26).

[5]It must be admitted, of course, that the severity and duration of suffering sometimes exceeds what seems to be required in order to bring people to moral and spiritual maturity.

[6]"Overall balance theodicies" are those that justify God for creating this sort of world by arguing that in the eschaton good will greatly outweigh evil. "Nonuniversalist theodicies" are those that deny that in the end everyone will enjoy eternal bliss with God in heaven. My own theodicy fits in both categories.

## Chapter 9: Can We Be Happy Apart from God?

[1]This chapter includes material adapted from Stephen T. Davis, "On Preferring That God Not Exist (Or That God Exist): A Dialogue," *Faith and Philosophy* 31, no. 2 (April 2014). Used by permission.

[2]Albert Camus, *The Stranger* (New York: Vintage, 1988), 121.

[3]Julian of Norwich, *Revelations of Divine Love*, trans. Clifton Wolters (London: Penguin Books, 1966), 103-4.

[4]This thought experiment is not original with me; it is based on something I read or heard many years ago (perhaps it is from C. S. Lewis or Francis Shafer), but I can no longer recall who to attribute it to.

[5]See Stephen T. Davis, "Resurrection, Personal Identity, and the Will of God," in *Personal Identity and Resurrection: How Do We Survive Our Death?* ed. Georg Gasser (Farnham, UK: Ashgate, 2010).

[6]See Stephen T. Davis, "Karma or Grace?" in *Christian Philosophical Theology* (Oxford: Oxford University Press, 2006).

## Conclusion

[1]Much of the second half of this chapter is based on Stephen T. Davis, "Conversion and the Rationality of Religion," in *Conversion*, ed. Ingolf U. Dalferth and Michael Ch. Rodgers (Tübingen, Germany: Mohr Siebeck, 2013). Used by permission.

[2]Pomona College was founded in 1887 by Congregationalists, but it has never been a Christian college.

[3]I did happen to encounter her again during the following academic year, and she reported that she was growing spiritually and that relations with her parents were not as difficult as she had anticipated.

[4]John Henry Newman, quoted in George Weigel, *Letters to a Young Catholic* (New York: Basic Books, 2015), 76.

[5]The "means of grace" are simply the ways in which we receive the grace of God, preeminently prayer, Scripture, worship, and the fellowship of brother and sister believers.

[6]I am a Presbyterian, and these questions are from the "Baptism of Adults" service from *The Book of Common Worship* (Philadelphia: Presbyterian Church in the USA, 1946).

[7]This claim is disputed by some in the current epistemological literature. I am taking the "steadfast" or "nonconformist" position on the topic of peer disagreement.

[8] Nicholas Wolterstorff, *Divine Discourse* (Cambridge: Cambridge University Press, 1995), 276.

[9] I introduced this distinction in Stephen T. Davis, *Faith, Skepticism, and Evidence* (Lewisburg, PA: Bucknell University Press, 1978), 26-28.

[10] Peter van Inwagen makes this point in "Quam Dilecta," in *God and the Philosophers*, ed. Thomas V. Morris (Oxford: Oxford University Press, 1994), 42-46.

[11] I should note that my criteria can equally apply to cases of conversion from religion to irreligion. Those sorts of conversions can be rational too.

[12] Kai Nielsen, *Philosophy and Atheism* (Buffalo, NY: Prometheus Books, 1985), 41.